"I am so grateful to God that Mark Vroegop has written this book. Far too often our discussions about racial harmony and reconciliation center on analysis, history, strategies, or the 'best practices' of those who have made some progress with regard to inclusion and diversity. What is overlooked is the primacy and power of empathy, 'weeping with those who weep.' This profound sense of identification is what the Bible calls lament. I am thankful to Vroegop for calling us to the heart of the matter—*our* hearts. *Weep with Me* is a gift and a treasure."

Crawford W. Loritts Jr., Senior Pastor, Fellowship Bible Church, Roswell, Georgia; author, *Unshaken*; Host, *Living a Legacy*

"If the sinful and tragic issues of racial injustice do not drive Christians to lament, it can only be because we do not, or will not, see the reality all around us. This book by the brilliant and faithful Mark Vroegop helps us to see that lament is not despair and resignation but instead the first step toward healing and restoration. This book will help Christians of every ethnicity to learn to love one another and to bear each other's burdens."

Russell Moore, President, The Ethics & Religious Liberty Commission of the Southern Baptist Convention

"When conversations on race and racial reconciliation seem to produce more heat than light, and more accusation than appreciation, Mark Vroegop provides a timely word in *Weep with Me*. He reveals the simple yet poignant power in the prayers of biblical lament, teaching us the need to weep with those who weep. Lament gives language to both speakers who've suffered and listeners who long to understand. This is the hope of lament and the hope of the book: that the language of lament would bring blessing out of brokenness. The author is neither a hopeless romantic nor a helpless idealist. With realistic expectations and unbridled hope, Vroegop conveys inspiration from the biblical language of lament to help us find ways that will promote trust, understanding, and hope. He has helped me to love, listen, and lament; to learn and to leverage. Reconciliation is never easy, yet because of the gospel of Jesus, I will still dare to hope."

Julius J. Kim, President, The Gospel Coalition; Professor of Practical Theology, Westminster Seminary California

"As a nation, we no longer know how to talk to each other about issues over which we disagree. Sadly, when it comes to issues of race or ethnicity, that inability has permeated the church. As a result, progress toward ethnic harmony appears to have slowed. But because we are in Christ, we can and should fight for the unity of the Spirit in the bond of peace. That's why I welcome Mark Vroegop's *Weep with Me*. He gives us a language we can use as we work together toward ethnic harmony. It's not a man-made language; it's the biblical language of lament. If your heart longs to see the church display the wisdom and glory of God to the cosmic powers, then you'll want to pick up this book, read it, practice it, and give it away. Let the conversations begin!"

Juan R. Sanchez, Senior Pastor, High Pointe Baptist Church, Austin, Texas

"Imagine if, in Jesus's story of the Pharisee and the publican (Luke 18:9–14), the publican, instead of repenting of his sins, had become offended by the Pharisee's assessment of him. Had that happened, you would have had two self-justifying sinners in the story, and we wouldn't have heard Jesus's beautiful declaration 'I tell you, this man [the publican] went down to his house justified.' So, please, if you are picking up this book in order to be offended, just don't. But if there is a weariness in your bones over your own sin and the sin of your people, and you long to see gospel unity and solidarity replace suspicion, separation, strife, division, indifference, ignorance, condescension, and contempt, come lament with me for a while, and pray. We are up against something only the Holy Spirit can fix, but he is more than a match for the challenge. Let's lament our hearts of stone and ask him to give us hearts of flesh (Ezek. 36:26–27). He can. He will."

Ligon Duncan, Chancellor and CEO, Reformed Theological Seminary

"*Weep with Me* is grounded in theology, informed by history, and saturated with humility. As a black member of Mark Vroegop's church, I have witnessed, primarily as an observer, how applying the biblical language of lament to racism has opened the door to reconciliation. Painful conversations between a white church leader and a black church member developed into a deep, trusting relationship. Intense early-morning discussions about race among a multiethnic group of leaders and members led to deeper understanding and biblical unity. A monthly discussion group exposed personal pain, yet weeping together increased shared knowledge and formed healthy relationships.

Casual multicultural interactions on Sundays led to meals together in each other's home. Civil Rights vision trips with the church exposed deep wounds and caused weeping among some and silence and confusion among others, but the language of lament led to enlightenment, caring, and mutual embrace as a reconciled body. Yes, the journey is difficult at times. No, we have not arrived at the dream. Through this book, Vroegop shows us how the language of lament leads to racial reconciliation. It is an encouraging read!"

A. Charles Ware, author; speaker; Founder and Executive Director, Grace Relations

"Mark Vroegop's earlier book, *Dark Clouds, Deep Mercy,* is the best book I have read on Christian lament. It moved me to preach through the book of Lamentations in my own church. Yet I was unprepared for how stirred I would be by the potential impact of Christian lament on racial tensions in the church today. But this is what Vroegop has done in *Weep with Me.* This book is a uniquely insightful contribution to a very difficult issue still largely ignored by modern-day evangelicals. It is a biblically faithful, immensely practical tool that guides us to a simple, clear solution to racial division in the church—empathy through Christian lament. Pastors especially need to read this book and use it to lead their congregations down a path of introspection rooted in the gospel and embodied in Christlike empathy toward all those in Christ. I highly commend this book and the faithful example of its author."

Brian Croft, Senior Pastor, Auburndale Baptist Church, Louisville, Kentucky; Founder, Practical Shepherding

"The challenges of racial division in America broadly and our churches specifically feel intractable. The conversation is riddled with indictment, hurt, anger, uncertainty, and fear. Yet Mark Vroegop offers a simple, mature, and biblical next step: learn the language of lament. Lament means one thing for the majority-culture Christian and a slightly different thing for the minority-culture Christian, and both lessons are crucial for preparing our hearts for understanding, forgiveness, reconciliation, and action. This book is excellent, and it's hard to imagine how churches will move toward racial reconciliation and the heavenly picture of unity in diversity apart from the biblical wisdom it provides."

Jonathan Leeman, Elder, Cheverly Baptist Church, Bladensburg, Maryland; Editorial Director, 9Marks

Also by Mark Vroegop

Dark Clouds, Deep Mercy: Discovering the Grace of Lament

WEEP WITH ME

How Lament Opens a Door for
Racial Reconciliation

Mark Vroegop

Foreword by Thabiti Anyabwile

∷ CROSSWAY®

WHEATON, ILLINOIS

Trade paperback ISBN: 978-1-4335-6759-9
ePub ISBN: 978-1-4335-6762-9
PDF ISBN: 978-1-4335-6760-5
Mobipocket ISBN: 978-1-4335-6761-2

Library of Congress Cataloging-in-Publication Data
Names: Vroegop, Mark, 1971– author. | Anyabwile, Thabiti M., 1970– writer of foreword.
Title: Weep with me : how lament opens a door for racial reconciliation / Mark Vroegop ; foreword by Thabiti Anyabwile.
Description: Wheaton, Illinois : Crossway, [2020] | Includes bibliographical references and index.
Identifiers: LCCN 2020000827 (print) | LCCN 2020000828 (ebook) | ISBN 9781433567599 (trade paperback) | ISBN 9781433567605 (pdf) | ISBN 9781433567612 (mobi) | ISBN 9781433567629 (epub)
Subjects: LCSH: Laments in the Bible. | Grief—Religious aspects—Christianity. | Suffering—Religious aspects—Christianity. | Race relations—Religious aspects—Christianity. | Reconciliation—Religious aspects—Christianity.
Classification: LCC BS1199.L27 V765 2020 (print) | LCC BS1199.L27 (ebook) DDC 277.308/3089—dc23
LC record available at https://lccn.loc.gov/2020000827
LC ebook record available at https://lccn.loc.gov/2020000828

Crossway is a publishing ministry of Good News Publishers.

BP   30   29   28   27   26   25   24   23   22   21   20
15   14   13   12   11   10   9   8   7   6   5   4   3   2   1

To Keith and Yolanda White

Fellow heirs of the gospel
Faithful followers of Jesus
Friends in the reconciliation journey

CONTENTS

FOREWORD

My family and I moved back to the United States from the Cayman Islands on July 1, 2014. We had just completed eight years of life and ministry in a country with over 110 nationalities living and working together on a strip of land just twenty-two miles by seven miles. Our church included well over thirty nationalities with no supermajority among us. It was the most diverse cultural context in which I'd ever lived and served.

Thirty-eight days after our arrival to the United States, Michael Brown was shot and killed in Ferguson, Missouri. Our furniture had not arrived from the Cayman Islands, so I sat on the carpeted stairs of our townhome watching news coverage on my iPad. I cannot adequately describe the surge of feelings—plural—that threatened to burst my heart as I watched coverage. There was grief over the death of Brown. There was anger as protesting crowds swelled. There was suspicion and resentment as first the police department and then the prosecutor seemed to bungle things. Changing stories produced confusion. But most of all there was fear for my then-seven-year-old son, born in the Cayman Islands, unschooled in the racial history and rules of the United States, ill-equipped for the inner-city realities he would now grow up in.

Then there came the emails and phone calls from well-intentioned pastor friends. Not to check on me or my son. But to tell me how wrong I was to have written this or said that. To assure me that "the narrative" I had "fallen for" was not true. To lecture me about respectability. To predict that my son would never face what Mike Brown faced because, well, he was my son.

Things got heated. Then some relationships frayed. Some others, sadly, ended in time.

As I look back on the couple of years that followed, it's clear to me that part of what was missing in those exchanges was a technology. Specifically, a language, a way of talking together that created doorways between very different experiences in our shared country. The need was evident in the numerous occasions white Christians asked, "How do we talk about these things?" The need was evident in the many occasions black Christians swore off ethnically mixed spaces. The need was evident when Latino/a and Asian brothers and sisters looked on quizzically, at once feeling left out or erased and yet longing to contribute.

We needed what Trekkies call a "universal translator." I can see the need for a common language clearly *now*, after reading this book. But then, in the heat of the many moments, I interpreted the "how" question in terms of content—what things to say or not say. But the book you hold in your hands has convinced me that the need wasn't content—there's plenty of that around—but process. We needed and still need a *way* of talking to each other. That way should encourage us to feel and express that feeling, create empathy, and turn us *together* toward God in faith.

As it turns out, our all-wise and all-loving God has given us in the Bible just such a technology, a way of talking with a built-in procedure and potential to help us express our feelings, empathize with others, turn to God in faith, and, by the Father's grace, inch toward a deeper experience of reconciliation. That way, that technology, that language is lament. Oh, that we would use this universal translator to commune with each other across our ethnic differences!

Mark Vroegop offers us an opportunity to grow in the practice and the promise of lament. In these pages you find the work of a practitioner. You can tell that, in some measure, Mark, like his Savior, is acquainted with grief. He knows something of the sorrow of others broken by the world's racial cruelties. He's acquainted because he's listened, empathized, turned to God in faith, and attempted real action. He's learned to lament with others.

Accessible. Biblical. Sensitive. Pastoral. Humble. Hopeful.

These are the things that characterize both the pastor-author and this book. In our always-talking world, we now have a book teaching us a different language to calm the clamor and instruct our tongues. It's not a book that attempts to fix everything or pretends its recommendations will be all the reader needs. But it's a start. A very good start. And really, a start at reconciliation is what most of the church needs.

I don't want to endure any more years of strife and turmoil like those following the shooting of Michael Brown. I don't want to lose another friend. I don't want to see the Lord's body split and torn any further by the mistrust and impatience Christians from different ethnic backgrounds sometimes exhibit. I'd far rather lament together. Mark has made me hopeful that lamenting together can help us live together. If you have or want that hope, too, turn the page and dig in.

Thabiti Anyabwile

ACKNOWLEDGMENTS

A book on racial reconciliation authored by a white pastor requires faithful and valiant people behind the scenes. This book would not be possible without a host of people I'd like to thank.

I've dedicated this book to Keith and Yolanda White, two African American church members who consistently model winsome and thoughtful engagement in racial reconciliation at a predominately white church. Their compassion, sacrifice, and perseverance inspire me to follow Jesus more faithfully. I regularly marvel at God's grace in them.

The leadership team of the Diversity Discipleship Discussion Group of College Park Church helped me lead a church-wide conversation about racial harmony. This ethnically diverse group of leaders has patiently answered my questions, provided insightful thoughts, and lovingly offered critiques when I've made mistakes. They created a monthly venue as a base camp for our church's growth in biblical unity. I'm thankful for the way God continues to use them in my life and our church.

The elders of College Park Church not only supported my writing but also navigated the messiness that comes with this topic. Their kind encouragement, eager teachability, and thoughtful questions made exploring this conversation possible.

A group of friends made this manuscript better by offering helpful suggestions and critiques: James Miles III, Dustin Crowe, Dale Shaw,

Jacki Halderman, Debbie Armbruster, Kris Abdnour, Stephen Lopez, Tim Whitney, Christel Taylor, Kenya Turner, Essence Brown, Isaac Adams, Joe Bartemus, and Jay and Marti Justice.

Thabiti Anyabwile models the kind of gracious clarity I hope to emulate in this book. His willingness to write the foreword and contribute an insightful lament not only provided an authoritative voice in racial harmony but, I'm sure, also encouraged other lament writers to add their voices as well.

I'm also grateful for the support of a team of literary professionals. Dave DeWit from Crossway once again leveraged his expertise and experience to make this book better—much better. Austin Wilson, from Wolgemuth and Associates, guided this book from concept to market. Thom Notaro tirelessly edited my manuscript, making my argument clearer.

Books are not written without enormous sacrifices of time. My wife, Sarah, released me to spend hours wrestling with words. She lovingly endured my verbal processing and joyfully embraced the invasion of another book into our family life. On a series of road trips, she patiently read chapters out loud, providing thoughtful insights and suggestions. Her relentless encouragement buoyed my heart through each stage of writing.

Finally, over a hundred people to date have embraced the risk of a pilgrimage called the Civil Rights Vision Trip. I've watched with wonder as transformation emerged through weeping with those who weep. The relationships, lament prayers, and new discoveries created a core group of people committed to pursuing biblical unity in diversity. I've seen reconciliation—one person at a time.

The grace and healing of those trips fueled the vision for this book.

I've witnessed lament open a door. I'm praying the door swings wide open.

Introduction

DREAM

The Vision of Racial Harmony

There is no institution more equipped and capable of bringing
transformation to the cause of reconciliation than the church.

JOHN PERKINS

"I want the church to look more like heaven."

How many times have you heard this statement about racial diversity in the church? It's a beautiful vision—people from all ethnicities worshiping together, loving one another, and living out their unity in Christ.

Imagine a sea of people—as far as your eyes can see—standing in front of Jesus. Everyone clothed with white robes and holding palm branches. Their anthem rolls like a crashing wave as they shout, "Salvation belongs to our God who sits on the throne, and to the Lamb!" With one voice they offer a glorious tribute to their Savior. Jesus stands alone as the victor. Sin is defeated. Satan is banished, redemption accomplished.

It's a scene from the seventh chapter of Revelation.

> After this I looked, and behold, a great multitude that no one
> could number, from every nation, from all tribes and peoples
> and languages, standing before the throne and before the Lamb,
> clothed in white robes, with palm branches in their hands, and
> crying out with a loud voice, "Salvation belongs to our God who
> sits on the throne, and to the Lamb!" (Rev. 7:9–10)

But what makes this scene compelling is not only the celebration; it's
the composition of the crowd.

This is an eternally assembled multitude, the saints from "every nation,
from all tribes and peoples and languages." A landscape of faces with various hues, beaming as they gaze upon Jesus. Imagine the beautiful tapestry
of skin color, the varying shades of ethnicity all assembled in the presence
of the King of kings: African, Hispanic, Asian, Native American, European, South American, and Pacific Islander. Hutus and Tutsis of Rwanda,
white and black Americans, Brahmins and Shudras in India, and white and
black South Africans all proclaiming their allegiance to the risen Christ.

Imagine historical divisions and prejudices gone. The pain of partiality and injustice healed. Superiority and pride erased. Standing
before the throne of God is a global and diverse multitude rescued by
a Jewish carpenter named Jesus. This was God's plan from the beginning. It's why Jesus died.

But shouldn't this unity in Christ be tasted now?

Weeping and Harmony

I've written this book because I'm compelled by the vision of ethnic
harmony through the gospel. Racial reconciliation is an essential part
of the church's story, and I'm grieved how far we are from it. You
probably picked up this book with a similar conviction and sadness.
Or perhaps you know things should be different, but you wonder
what we can do.

I'd like to invite you to join me in helping the church look more like heaven—right now. And I'm going to suggest a place to start: lament. The biblical language of empathy and exile, perseverance and protest, can open the door for reconciliation. By learning to weep with those who weep we can take steps toward living in harmony with one another (Rom. 12:15–16). As you'll see, lament won't solve all the problems. But it can help.

You might think the church looking more like heaven now seems like a dream—maybe even a fairy tale.

But it happened before.

Divided City, United Church

Followers of Jesus were first called "Christians" in Antioch (Acts 11:26). The term means "those belonging to Christ."[1] However, the name that now defines over a third of the world and two billion people was not self-selected. Other people called the disciples of Jesus "Christians." Have you ever wondered why?

Ethnic harmony was part of the story.

Antioch thrived as a metropolitan city with people from a variety of ethnicities and backgrounds. Like many Roman cities, it was segregated by design. At the establishment of Antioch in 300 BC a wall separated Syrian people from Greek people.[2] As the city grew under Roman domination, eighteen ethnic groups divided its population.[3] As in many cities in the empire, ethnic division and violence were common.[4] Segregation was their solution. Sound familiar?

A thriving church blossomed in Antioch. Historians are not certain who planted this assembly, but it became the launching pad for

---

1. John B. Polhill, *Acts*, vol. 26 of *The New American Commentary* (Nashville: Broadman & Holman, 1992), 273.

2. Rodney Stark, *The Rise of Christianity: How the Obscure, Marginal Jesus Movement Became the Dominant Religious Force in the Western World in a Few Centuries* (New York: HarperOne, 1996), 157.

3. *The Archaeological Encyclopedia of the Holy Land*, ed. Avraham Negev, 3rd ed. (New York: Prentice Hall, 1990), s.v. "Antioch-on-the-Orontes."

4. Stark, *The Rise of Christianity*, 158.

the spread of the gospel to the uttermost parts of the earth (Matt. 28:18–20). The book of Acts demonstrates the strategic and transformative influence of the church in Antioch. The church experienced an inexplicable unity forged by the gospel.

That's why a new name—"Christian"—was needed.

New People

The church at Antioch wasn't Jewish. It wasn't Gentile. It was both. That was new. Regardless of ethnicity, these believers united around their common belief in the death and resurrection of Jesus Christ. Unity in the gospel flourished in the church. Culture and ethnicity no longer separated them. Their allegiance to Jesus and love for one another created a countercultural community.

The world had no category for them.

This was only the beginning. Racial unity through the gospel spread beyond Antioch. About three hundred miles away, the church in Colossae received these words from the apostle Paul: "Here [in the church] there is not Greek and Jew, circumcised and uncircumcised, barbarian, Scythian, slave, free; but Christ is all, and in all" (Col. 3:11). As the gospel impacted the hearts of God's people, it changed how they related to each other around the world. In the book of Galatians we read, "There is neither Jew nor Greek, there is neither slave nor free, there is no male and female, for you are all one in Christ Jesus" (Gal. 3:28).

Spiritual oneness in Christ became the hallmark of the church.

Underneath the most visible demarcations of ethnicity, a more fundamental identity emerged. Jesus brought people together.

Gospel unity created racial harmony.

Old Problem

Sounds incredible, doesn't it? I think most believers agree that biblical unity is something to pray for and work toward. You probably picked up this book knowing that reconciliation between a diverse group of people is a beautiful dream.

But is the church marked by a compelling ethnic unity today? Do you know how to make progress toward racial reconciliation?

Unfortunately, the kind of oneness championed in the New Testament and modeled in the early church feels like it's a long way off. If we're honest, we have to admit that the American church is still marked by deep ethnic division.

It's a long, sad story.

I'm sure you've heard that "the most segregated hour in America is 11:00 o'clock on Sunday morning." Tragically, the effects of hundreds of years of slavery and the legacy of segregation created canyons of pain and distrust. Additionally, the political, social, and media landscape fossilized our divisions, creating echo chambers of information and opinions. Instead of building bridges toward one another, it feels as if racial fissures are growing wider and deeper—even within the evangelical church. On the whole, churches in America don't look like Antioch.

If we're honest, it's hurt our witness.

Our culture is not marveling at our brotherhood across ethnic fault lines. No one feels the need to create a new name for Christians because of our otherworldly unity. Additionally, most Christians aren't sure what to do about it.

Many of us don't know how to talk about it. We are understandably nervous about discussing racial reconciliation because there are so many land mines. Words must be chosen carefully, and we fear saying the wrong thing. Sometimes we retreat from hard conversations because we don't know what to say. All it takes is a video on Facebook highlighting a racial incident, blunt words from a minority friend, a battle on social media, or a theological discussion on justice, and the fear and division deepen.

What's more, when brothers or sisters are wounded by racial insensitivity or mistreatment, they may not know how to express their hurt without being misunderstood or marginalized. Perhaps expressing sorrow has resulted in being maligned or accused of playing the "race card." They might conclude it's better to bury the pain—again. Without compassion from fellow believers, frustration or bitterness easily takes root.

The chasm between believers widens.

Part of the problem is that our dream of racial harmony is ahead of our language. The evangelical church still hasn't found its common voice. At least not yet.

What if we could take a step in that direction?

A Starting Point

The aim of this book is to give the church a language that moves Christians of different ethnicities toward reconciliation. In the chapters that follow, I hope you'll learn to be fluent in lament, the historic prayer language of processing and expressing grief.

I'd like to show you how lament opens a door for racial reconciliation.

Now, I'm not so naive as to think that learning to lament will fix all the problems connected to racial divisions in the church and in the culture. I merely believe this biblical language is a helpful starting point.

Too often discussions about racial reconciliation tip toward political talking points, or arguments about statistics and history. We tend to become defensive, rehearsing all-too-common narratives from our hurt or experiences. Often the volume and vitriol are elevated. I'd like to strike a different tone, a unifying language amid our differing personal histories, perceptions, and struggles.

I've titled this book *Weep with Me* with the hope we can learn to apply Romans 12:15–16: "Weep with those who weep. Live in harmony with one another." I've applied these concepts in my life and my church as we've stumbled our way toward greater unity and racial reconciliation. While we have much to learn and a lot of room for growth, I've witnessed what happens when Christians start with lament.

Prayers in pain lead to trust—together. Tears, love, and unity replace misunderstanding, distrust, and hurt. We get glimpses of a heavenly unity.

A Hopeful Journey

Learning the language of lament is a journey.

This book is divided into three parts. In part 1 we'll start with a basic definition of terms and learn what the biblical language of lament involves. Then we'll discover the value of spirituals, a musical expression of lament in American culture. And I'll also show you why I think lament opens a door for reconciliation.

Parts 2 and 3 focus on the application of lament. In part 2 we'll learn how lament can help white Christians weep, speak, and repent where needed. In part 3 we'll explore lament for African American and other minority believers as they wrestle with exile, redeem their hurt, and dare to hope again. Finally, we'll conclude by looking at the implications of what we've learned together.

I've chosen three topics for each group. I don't mean to imply that they are not broadly applicable to all believers regardless of ethnicity. Lament is fluid enough and brokenness deep enough for a wide array of expression. However, I think lament is helpful in racial reconciliation as it is applied uniquely in each group's given context, history, or need.

Since I'm writing to a broad array of readers, I quote from a variety of authors who approach racial reconciliation differently. My research uncovered a diversity of perspectives and worldviews. I've cited material I found helpful, but you should not assume that I agree with everything a particular author writes if his or her work is listed in the bibliography. Exploring racial reconciliation requires balance and wisdom to listen to different viewpoints while still charting a biblically faithful path forward.

You'll also see that each chapter concludes with a prayer of lament by a national leader. The prayer contributors graciously agreed to add their unique voices so you can learn from their examples as you read their laments. The goal is to inspire you to pray your own laments as you ponder their prayers.

By the end of this book I hope you'll know how to start on a path toward racial reconciliation and see glimpses of a heavenly unity in your life and in the church.

One Voice

In the book of Romans deep disagreements based upon culture, backgrounds, and preferences threatened to divide the church. They created an unwelcoming culture among members. Battle lines were drawn. Tribes formed. Emotions ran high. Paul called them to a bigger vision:

> May the God of endurance and encouragement grant you to live in such harmony with one another, in accord with Christ Jesus, that together you may with one voice glorify the God and Father of our Lord Jesus Christ. Therefore welcome one another as Christ has welcomed you, for the glory of God. (Rom. 15:5–7)

Welcoming one another. Living in harmony. Glorifying the Father with one voice. Reflecting the unity of the triune Godhead.

That's the vision: a diverse and united church.

John Perkins, civil rights activist and author of *One Blood*, believes the church is the best place for racial reconciliation. He writes: "There is no institution more equipped and capable of bringing transformation to the cause of reconciliation than the church. But we have some hard work to do."[5] I think he's right.

Lament is where we can begin.

Christianity looks stunning to the world and most emulates Jesus when our identity and unity in the gospel are more foundational than any other identity—including our ethnicity. Our

---

5. John Perkins, *One Blood: Parting Words to the Church on Race and Love* (Chicago: Moody Publishers, 2018), 63.

broken world needs to see this vision lived out in new and fresh ways in the church.

While lament doesn't solve all the problems, it's a place to begin. For the sake of racial reconciliation, I'm inviting you to embrace a bigger, heavenly vision.

Come, weep with me.

◊

LAMENT PRAYER

O Lord, how long will your church be divided along racial lines? How long will the lingering effects of animosity, injustice, and pride mark your blessed bride? How long, O Lord, will my white brothers and sisters not understand the pain in those whose experience is different than ours? How long, O Lord, will my minority brothers and sisters struggle with distrust and feel ostracized?

God, grant us the heart to weep with those who weep. Give us empathy and understanding. Create trust where there is pain. Make your church the united bride you want her to be.

These divisions of mistrust and historical bias run deep, O God. Without you, nothing will ever change. In our pain and our weariness, we express our hope that Jesus can change our hearts and unite the church. We believe the gospel is greater than our divisions. And we long for the day when the world will take note of how we love each other. So, help us to meet each other in this prayerful journey. We come to learn to lament. Hear us as we weep together, that we might walk together.

In the name of Jesus, our King. Amen.

Mark Vroegop,
lead pastor of College Park Church,
Indianapolis, Indiana

Discussion Questions

1. If you were to ask an unbeliever in your city what he or she thinks about race relations in "the church," what words do you think that person would use? Why would he or she select those words?

2. Describe the kind of church experience you had growing up as it relates to racial reconciliation. If you were not raised in church, describe the culture in your family or city when it came to ethnicity.

3. What fears do you have as you read this book? What makes you nervous?

4. How familiar are you with the biblical category of lament? What do you think it means to lament?

5. Why is it important for the church to work toward racial reconciliation? What happens if this is neglected?

6. List three to five prayer requests for yourself and your church as you enter this journey.

PART 1

LAMENT IN THE BIBLE AND HISTORY

1

PRAY

The Language of Lament

Not my brother, not my sister, but it's me, O Lord,
Standin' in the need of prayer. . . .
It's me, it's me, O Lord,
Standin' in the need of prayer.

AFRICAN AMERICAN SPIRITUAL

My journey in reconciliation started with tears in an African American pastor's office.

A providential meeting nearly thirty years ago changed me.

After college I worked as an admissions counselor for a Christian university. My responsibilities included meeting with inner-city African American pastors with hopes of their high school students applying to our college. Unfortunately, the student body of this conservative, historically Baptist college wasn't multiethnic. Not even close.

However, the university implemented some important steps. I was part of the team trying to recruit Christian students from other ethnicities. I scheduled an introductory meeting with a leading African American pastor. Our diversity director joined me.

The pastor sat behind an impressive oak desk and was dressed in a perfectly tailored suit with a face radiating strength and grace. His warm, booming voice commanded respect.

After explaining the purpose of our visit, I asked him why more of his students didn't apply to our Christian university. My naivete was surely obvious. He was gracious.

The pastor explained the barriers his kids faced: the challenges of inner-city life, educational disparities, and generational poverty. He told me the issue was not as simple as I assumed—there were problems that made it extremely difficult for his kids to consider applying, let alone enrolling in our college. He said, "My kids simply do not have the same opportunities as the students who attend your university."

The argument was not new to me. But I had never heard it directly from someone who expressed it so clearly.

My Dutch Heritage

Before I explain what happened next, you need to know about my family background. My paternal grandparents and father were born in the Netherlands. After World War II, the Vroegops immigrated to the United States with five children. A farmer on the East Coast paid their passage in return for several years of service.

After paying their debts, my grandparents and father settled in Kalamazoo, Michigan. Family connections and a network of Dutch-speaking friends helped them navigate a new country. My grandfather worked for anyone who would employ him, including a garbage company for a while. It's an amazing story, the Amercian dream.

Sadly, my grandfather died fifteen months before I was born. While I didn't have the privilege of a relationship with him, a particular worldview was part of my inheritance. Here's the narrative: The United States is a land of opportunity. If you are disciplined, work hard, stay married, and live frugally, the United States is full of opportunities. I don't remember being taught this cultural script. But this Dutch worldview was foundational.

A Tear-Filled Awakening

Back to the pastor's office.

His statement "My kids simply do not have the same opportunities as the students who attend your university" struck a nerve. I pushed back with an oft rehearsed narrative: "Pastor, with all due respect, I don't understand why you would say kids in your church lack opportunity. This nation is filled with opportunities." I recounted the story of my grandfather.

The pastor paused. I actually thought I had convinced him. This narrative, after all, was inarguable. But my perspective was about to be challenged.

I didn't see it coming.

He leaned toward me, speaking graciously and slowly. It seemed like he'd had this conversation before. "I'm sure your grandfather worked hard. But here's the thing: your grandfather was able to get a job in the 1940s. The color of his skin didn't create any barriers. Do you think my black grandfather could have been hired for the same job as your white grandfather in the 1940s?" He paused, waiting for my answer.

My mind quickly ran through the history of my hometown. I knew the division. I heard the jokes. I knew the mantra "If you're not Dutch, you're not much."

The answer was obvious.

"No, sir, he would not," I quietly replied.

The pastor now made his point clear: "Mark, think of the difference that made. Ask yourself how much of your life is connected to the simple fact that your grandfather came to the United States as a white man."

Suddenly, I saw the world through a different lens. It grieved me. Why didn't I see it before?

That's when the tears started.

Overcome with surprising sorrow, I sat in the chair quietly weeping. I was ashamed of my arrogance, and overwhelmed with the pain I saw in the pastor's eyes. Stunned by the implications of what I heard, I couldn't speak.

My reaction startled my colleague from the university. She asked, "Pastor, what's happening right now?"

He said, "Sister, our brother has just seen something he's never seen before."

He was right.

While laws and cultural norms had changed since the 1940s, I never fully considered the present implications of the past, or the existing hurdles and barriers that minorities might face. My family story made it easy for me to ignore the experiences of others. I had never engaged—face-to-face—with someone struggling with a different context than mine. To be clear: I wasn't wrestling with "white guilt." My eyes were opened to the narrowness of my cultural narrative, but also to my lack of compassion. That's what hit me. And it grieved me—deeply.

I left with a changed heart. The meeting in the pastor's office became a defining moment. My first lament about race came unexpectedly. It felt like a conversion.

It was the beginning of a lifelong journey.

Discovering Lament

My first book, *Dark Clouds, Deep Mercy: Discovering the Grace of Lament*, explores the nuances of lament in the Psalms and Lamentations for walking through grief. In God's providence, writing about lament and a movement of diversity in our church ran on parallel paths. What began as a small group of minority leaders talking with our pastors about racial reconciliation blossomed into a shift in the composition and culture of our mostly white church in the suburbs of Indianapolis. Our church, like every church, is far from perfect. It's been messy. But we've seen God move.

This book, *Weep with Me*, developed as I observed unique applications of lament to racial reconciliation. I've witnessed not only how lament serves people wrestling with loss but also how it gives people a language for talking to God and to one another about the pain and sorrow hindering racial reconciliation.

I became convinced that lament, as a biblical prayer language, can open a door for reconciliation. When Christians from majority and minority cultures learn to grieve together, they reaffirm their common bond as brothers and sisters in Christ. Lament enters into the deep emotions of sorrow, hurt, misunderstanding, and injustice.

When it comes to racial reconciliation, I think we should approach the conversation as we would if a dear friend experienced a deep loss. Our first step should be to sit beside the grieving individual. Love the person. Listen. And lament with him or her. Bryan Loritts offers this helpful advice:

> The way forward is not an appeal to the facts as a first resort. Rather, we should attempt to get inside each other's skin as best as we can to feel what they feel and understand it. . . . Basically, there are five levels of communication: 1. Cliché; 2. Facts; 3. Opinion; 4. Feelings; 5. Transparency, with "cliché" representing the shallowest form of communication and "transparency" the deepest. I will never know what it's like to be a woman, but I do know that when my wife comes at me with level four (feelings), and I stay in lawyer-land at level two, this never is a recipe for intimacy. I am not denying facts, but I've had to learn the hard way that if I am to experience oneness with my bride, I must drop down to level four in an attempt to understand before I resurface to level two. Facts are a first and last resort in a court of law, but

when it comes to human relationships, let us first stop and feel before we go to facts.[1]

Lament starts with a humble posture. It communicates: "I'm here. I'm sad too. Let's talk to Jesus, because we need his help."

Lament is not the only step. Developing relationships, honest conversations, discussions about perceptions, and working for change must also be part of the reconciliation process. As I learned in the pastor's office, society at large can create barriers that still negatively affect our culture, relationship networks, and opportunities. There's much work to do. Lament isn't a simplistic solution.

But I've seen how it helps.

Definitions

Before we explore lament and racial reconciliation, we need to define a few terms. Clarifying the meaning of words will help us avoid confusion.

I'm a white Christian pastor with a Dutch heritage. I'm writing to people who share the same skin color as mine and to those who don't. I hope to apply lament to both groups. But what do we call these two categories of readers? We don't have descriptions that apply well in every context. At the same time, we need to know whom I'm writing to or about.

Majority and Minority Cultures

For the purposes of this book I will use *majority culture* to refer to those of us who are white. I will use the term *minority culture* as a category for African Americans, Latino Americans, Asian Americans, and other people groups who have historically not been a part of "the majority" in the United States. I realize that the majority/

---

1. Ed Stetzer, "It's Time to Listen: Feeling the Pain Despite the Facts, a Guest Post by Bryan Loritts," *Christianity Today*, August 20, 2014, https://www.christianitytoday.com/edstetzer/2014/august/its-time-to-listen.html.

minority distinction may not be statistically accurate in certain parts of the country. Further, they will not likely be useful terms in the future as demographics change. I'm using the distinction merely in its historical context while acknowledging the limitations of the terms.

Throughout this book I will refer to minorities with a particular application to African American or black Christians. I don't intend to exclude other minority groups. I'm merely attempting to apply lament to the most prominent historical division—between white and black Christians. I know there are other challenges. I hope that by focusing on the white-black reconciliation issue, other applications will follow.

Race

The term *race* is also important to define. First, we need to acknowledge that the Bible talks about one race—the human race. Every man or woman reflects the same image of God (Gen. 1:26). When the Bible distinguishes between people, it is on the basis of ethnicity: "tribes and peoples and languages" (Rev. 7:9). I prefer the term *ethnicity* because it's closer to the biblical text and it connects people to their geographic and cultural origins.

However, the term *race* is more commonly used in our culture. We need to understand the background of this term. Race, in American history, is a social construct. In other words, our society created the term and defined it. Race deconstructed ethnicity (European, African, Asian, etc.) into two categories merely related to the color of one's skin: white and black ("colored"). White became an all-encompassing category based on the color of one's skin—not ethnicity. What's more, the creation of the term was associated with superiority and white supremacy.

Tragically, the roots of race can be traced back to the grievous sin of slavery. Daniel Hill explains:

The horror of slavery was a major moral crisis for America, but instead of acknowledging the sin of that enterprise, we went in the opposite direction. We began to deemphasize the differences within various European ethnicities and began to describe white people as a human collective that was inherently superior to people of color.[2]

Racism

What about *racism*? This word takes the definition of *race* and systematizes the ideology of superiority/inferiority in language, laws, and culture. Racism treats people unfairly based upon the belief of their inferiority. Prejudice is different. It's the negative beliefs and attitudes toward a person based upon his or her association with a group. It's painting broadly with a negative bias. Racism uses skin color for sinful partiality (see James 2:1–13). And in racist cultures, it combines superiority and power into a repressive system.

Let me give you an example. If you traced the immigration patterns of the Irish to America, you would learn that in their early years Irish immigrants were treated as inferior to other European ethnic groups. Because of their suffering, the Irish formed a unique bond with African Americans. In fact, in the census of 1850, the term *mulatto* was introduced for the first time, in part because of children who were of Irish and African American descent.

Irish immigration overlapped with the development of the social construct of race in the nineteenth century. The Irish lived in the same neighborhoods and competed for the same jobs as blacks. Since the Irish wanted to be accepted as white, they eventually embraced racism against African Americans. In essence, the Irish became white. Their ethnicity was eclipsed by race. The racism within the culture of the United States allowed them to do this.[3] And they were not alone.

---

2. Daniel Hill, *White Awake: An Honest Look at What It Means to Be White* (Downers Grove, IL: InterVarsity Press, 2017), 51.

3. Hill, *White Awake*, 51–52.

These definitions are loaded, aren't they? You probably feel the tension. You may have some questions. However, remember that the church is a great place for racial reconciliation because we have an identity underneath the most painful categories in our culture. In Christ we find the resources to have this conversation since our identity in the gospel undergirds and informs our history, ethnicity, and culture—even our "race."

With that in mind, let's learn about lament to see how vital it is for racial reconciliation.

Defining *Lament*

Simply stated, a lament is a prayer in pain that leads to trust. Laments are more than merely the expression of sorrow. The goal of a lament is to recommit oneself to hoping in God, believing his promises, and a godly response to pain, suffering, and injustice.

Lament is the historic biblical prayer language of Christians in pain. It's the voice of God's people while living in a broken world. Laments acknowledge the reality of pain while trusting in God's promises.

Over a third of the Psalms are laments. They talk to God about the paradox of God's promises and the presence of pain. Sometimes the lament is personal. At other times it is a prayer for an entire group. Sometimes lament prayers reflect repentance. And some psalms of lament express sorrow and frustration over injustice.

The breadth of situations in which laments are prayed make it uniquely helpful.

The book of Lamentations laments the destruction of Jerusalem as people cling to hope in God. The prophet Jeremiah refused to allow his heart to crumble when he looked at the rubble of the city.

> The thought of my suffering and homelessness
> 　is bitter beyond words.

I will never forget this awful time,
    as I grieve over my loss.
Yet I still dare to hope
    when I remember this:

The faithful love of the LORD never ends!
    His mercies never cease. (Lam. 3:19–22 NLT)

Lament enters the complicated space of deep disappointment and lingering hurt. It boldly reaffirms the trustworthiness of God.

Basics of Lament

Now that you understand the concept, we need to learn how to lament. Let me briefly highlight four elements.

Turn to God

Laments talk to God about pain.[4] Confusion, exhaustion, and disappointment can cause us to retreat from the one who knows our sorrows. The poisonous mist of bitterness or anger can sweep in, creating a fog of unbelief or a justification for ungodly behavior.

Lament talks to God even if it's messy. This requires faith. Silence is easier but unhealthy. Lament prays through hardship. Consider the gut-level honesty of Psalm 77:

I cry aloud to God,
    aloud to God, and he will hear me.
In the day of my trouble I seek the Lord;
    in the night my hand is stretched out without wearying;
    my soul refuses to be comforted.
When I remember God, I moan;
    when I meditate, my spirit faints. (vv. 1–3)

---

4. This and the following three points draw upon my article "How Lament Is a Path to Praise," Crosswalk, March 25, 2019, https://www.crosswalk.com/faith/spiritual-life/how-lament-is-a-path-to-praise.html. See also Mark Vroegop, *Dark Clouds, Deep Mercy: Discovering the Grace of Lament* (Wheaton, IL: Crossway, 2019).

Even though hope feels distant, lamenters reach out to God. This historic prayer language invites us to keep crying out in prayer.

Complain

The second step in lament candidly talks to God about what is wrong. Biblical complaint vocalizes circumstances that do not seem to fit with God's character or his purposes. While the psalmist knows God is in control, there are times when it feels like he's not. When it seems that injustice rules the day, lament invites us to talk to God about it. Instead of stuffing our struggles, lament gives us permission to verbalize the tension. Psalm 13 wrestles with why God isn't doing more:

> How long, O LORD? Will you forget me forever?
>> How long will you hide your face from me?
> How long must I take counsel in my soul
>> and have sorrow in my heart all the day?
> How long shall my enemy be exalted over me? (vv. 1–2)

Biblical complaining is not venting your sinful anger. It's merely telling God about your struggles. And the more honest we can be, the sooner we are able to move to the next element.

Ask

Lament seeks more than relief; it yearns for the deliverance that fits with God's character. Godly lamenters keep asking even when the answer is delayed.

> Consider and answer me, O LORD my God;
>> light up my eyes, lest I sleep the sleep of death,
> lest my enemy say, "I have prevailed over him,"
>> lest my foes rejoice because I am shaken. (Ps. 13:3–4)

Lament affirms the applicability of God's promises by asking again and again for divine help. Repeated requests become hopeful reminders of what God can do. Asking boldly serves to strengthen our resolve to not give up. But it also encourages us to embrace the destination of all lament: a renewal of trust.

Trust

Confidence in God's trustworthiness is the destination of all laments. Turning, complaining, and asking lead here. Laments help us through suffering by directing our hearts to make the choice—often daily— to trust in God's purposes hidden behind the pain. In this way, a lament is one of the most theologically informed practices of the Christian life.

Laments lead us through our sorrows so that we can trust God and praise him. This is how Psalm 13 concludes. Notice the pivot on the word "but" and the direct decision to trust, rejoice, and sing:

> But I have trusted in your steadfast love;
>> my heart shall rejoice in your salvation.
> I will sing to the LORD,
>> because he has dealt bountifully with me. (vv. 5–6)

It's a powerful ending to a blunt and honest psalm. Every lament is designed to become this kind of pathway toward hopeful godliness.

These four elements (turning, complaining, asking, and trusting) serve as the basic ingredients of lament. Since biblical laments are poems set to music, they don't always include every element. But this framework provides the structure for talking to God and praying together about the brokenness of the world.

When it comes to the historic scar of racism and a lack of reconciliation, lament can be a helpful language to learn.

A Common Language

In racial reconciliation, a common language unites people. When the hip-hop artist Jay-Z was interviewed by Oprah Winfrey, he made a stunning statement:

Hip-hop has done more for racial relations than most cultural icons. . . .

This music didn't only influence kids from urban areas, it influenced people all around the world. . . .

If you look at clubs and how integrated they have become—before people partied in separate clubs. There were hip-hop clubs and there were techno clubs. And now people party together and once you have people partying, dancing, and singing along to the same music, then conversations naturally happen after that. And within conversations, we all realize that we're more alike than we are separate.[5]

From a secular standpoint, I think Jay-Z is right. Hip-hop created a language that opens doors between people of different ethnicities. And when that happens, reconciliation is more likely.

Biblical lament does the same thing.

Where Lament Fits

Racial reconciliation is a process. Lament can be redemptive. I have found it helpful to think about lament in the context of a fivefold path: love, listen, lament, learn, and leverage. Let me explain each of these steps.

Love

The church should be involved in racial reconciliation because of what we believe. Our common relationship with Jesus, regardless of our ethnicity, creates a new spiritual identity. We are part of the same family. We bear God's image. We love the same Savior. This is more foundational than any cultural or racial category—"Christ is all, and in all" (Col. 3:11; see also 3:14–17). Racial reconciliation flows from this Christ-centered identity. Christians start with love because of the gospel.

---

5. Eric Mason, "How Should the Church Engage?," in *The Gospel and Racial Reconciliation*, ed. Russell Moore and Andrew T. Walker (Nashville: B&H, 2016), 53–54.

Listen

The second step relates to James 1:19: "Let every person be quick to hear, slow to speak, slow to anger." James attempted to help a church navigate ongoing conflicts and live spiritually mature lives. I'm sure you'll agree with me that this biblical principle applies in many areas. It has unique applications to discussions about racial tension and ethnic reconciliation. Too often the tone of the conversation is marked by closed minds, hasty words, and angry attitudes. However, if we can commit to a posture of listening without speaking quickly or getting angry, irritated, or frustrated, there's hope for progress.

Lament

We've already started learning about lament, and the rest of this book explores this critical step, so I won't spend much time here. Suffice it to say that lament helps us by giving us steps toward future progress. It supplies a biblical voice that allows us to talk to God and one another about the pain we feel and see. As you'll see in the chapters to come, it opens a door for reconciliation.

Learn

The fourth step is a commitment to learn from one another. Our cultural backgrounds, understandings of history, and experiences create assumptions and blind spots. If we take the posture of learning from one another, we create a safe environment for asking questions and working through disagreements. But we also discover new concepts or even historical realities we didn't fully understand. As I've entered into the pursuit of racial reconciliation, I can't tell you how many times I've said: "I had no idea. Why didn't I know this?" We are able to grow by learning from one another, allowing the diversity of experience and perspectives to make us wiser and more mature.

Leverage

The final step involves action and change. The goal of racial reconciliation is not merely to pray about what's wrong or to express our empathy. Our minority brothers and sisters grow weary of efforts that stop here. The vision for this book is for these steps, including lament, to bring change—in our hearts, our churches, and our culture. Depending on your context, you'll have to determine what that looks like. It could include creating new relationships, speaking up when racially insensitive comments are made, practicing intentional hospitality, talking with your church leadership about reconciliation, or reading a wider array of books. You might find ways to increase the ethnic diversity around your dinner table, at your workplace, or in your church. If you're a minority, it might look like practicing a heart of love and kindness toward hurtful people or choosing to share your pain from racial insensitivity or injustice. I'll provide other examples in the chapters that follow. The key is to understand that racial reconciliation requires action. Love, listening, lamenting, and learning are designed to lead us here.

This fivefold model gives us a framework to consider how to pursue ethnic harmony. Lament can be a vital part of the reconciliation process. The gospel is more foundational than our most painful historical categories. "Here there is not Greek and Jew, circumcised and uncircumcised, barbarian, Scythian, slave, free; but Christ is all, and in all" (Col. 3:11). Lament prayerfully reinforces this Christ-centered identity. It's the voice of humility and empathy.

It opens a door for reconciliation.

My conversation with the African American pastor was the beginning of a journey. A lot of learning, conversations, tears, and mistakes happened along the way. But God used that brief conversation to begin something in me. Lament was an important part of the process.

I hope you'll join me in this journey.

LAMENT PRAYER

How long, O Lord, will you leave us in our blindness? Won't you open our eyes and our hearts to each other? The minds of your people are not renewed as they ought to be. We cling to American cultural patterns and myths that ignore or deny the painful stories of others. We remain ignorant of the ways race and color have opened opportunity for some while closing it for others. We choose to reject the knowledge of these histories and injustices so that we might protect our own fragile identities and self-regard. We refuse to acknowledge the prejudice, bigotry, racism, and oppression that is obviously behind and before us. How long, O Lord, will you leave us in blindness?

Father in heaven, enlighten the eyes of our understanding. Your church fails at times to live together in love and empathy. We fail to enter one another's shoes. We prefer the self-fulfilling prophecies of national narratives, the privilege of our protective cultures, the comfort of our cultural companions, the power of our political tribes. We count the risk of loving "others" too costly a gamble to make. How long, O Lord, before we practice the human and humanizing spiritual disciplines of sitting with and listening to each other?

O Lord, the pain of our many rejections, the wounds of our many withdrawals, the isolation of our many suspicions have weakened our unity, our witness, and our love. But you love us, and you have promised to finish the work you began in us. You have predestined us to be conformed to the image of your Son. Grant that the same love with which Christ loved us might be shared abundantly between Christians of every hue, history, culture, class, and language. O great God our Father, fill your household with Christ's redemptive love!

Thabiti Anyabwile,
pastor of Anacostia River Church,
Washington, DC

Discussion Questions

1. When it comes to discussing the topic of race, what are the immediate fears, concerns, or questions you have?

2. What is your ethnic and cultural background, and how did it shape your understanding of the world?

3. Review the definition of lament and the four elements. What makes sense to you about lament? What is unclear?

4. Without knowing the rest of the book, how can you imagine lament helping in the conversation about racial reconciliation?

5. Review the five steps of reconciliation (love, listen, lament, learn, and leverage). Which is the hardest for you to understand and apply? What steps can you take to grow?

6. Using a lament psalm (see appendix 1), see if you can identify the four elements.

7. Write your own lament about any kind of pain or suffering in your life. Then write a lament about the subject of race and ethnic divisions.

2

LISTEN

Lessons from African American Spirituals

The Psalms allow us to listen in on the soul's
anguish; the spirituals do the same.

DANTE STEWART

"Why do you think the evangelical church doesn't understand lament?"

The question was part of a video interview for my previous book. It's a good question. While a third of the Psalms are lament-oriented, contemporary hymns and songs are generally lament-lite. However, the question illustrated a common misunderstanding about lament, church history, and traditions.

"Can I reframe your question?" I asked.

We should ask: "Why does the white evangelical church not understand lament? If we look to the African American church tradition, we'll find lots of lament. In fact, the leading category of lament in American history would be the spirituals."

This is not the only time that I've reframed the question about lament in the context of the church. I think the need to do so tells us two things. First, our perspective is often limited to circles in which we've worshiped. It's easy to draw sweeping conclusions based upon the slice of our experience—what we've seen, heard, sung, or read.

Second, it is important to step outside our cultural sphere and listen to the experiences and lessons from believers from different backgrounds. This is where African American spirituals[1] are uniquely helpful. These songs of sorrow expressed the emotional trauma of slavery and segregation. They protested exile created by the sins of partiality and abuse. By considering them, we identify with the pain of racial injustice. We memorialize important lessons about suffering and hardship from fellow believers. And we are better able to empathize with the present hurts and challenges our minority brothers and sisters face.

Listening through Lament

In this chapter, I want to help you take some first steps toward reconciliation through listening. We'll examine the connection between lament, spirituals, and racial harmony. The spirituals provide rich history and important truths. I'm intentionally placing this chapter early because of the fivefold vision for conversations about racial reconciliation (love, listen, lament, learn, and leverage). If we don't begin with the right posture, no amount of information or discussion will help.

Before we look at the spirituals, let's consider three ways laments help us listen, especially when it comes to racial reconciliation.

Vocalize the Pain

Lament provides Christians with a common language to talk about pain. Since over a third of the Psalms feature this minor-key song, it gives us permission to talk to God—either in private or together—

---

1. Sometimes these songs are called Negro or African American spirituals. For the sake of both consistency and sensitivity, I will simply use the term *spirituals* for this genre.

about the pain we feel. When it comes to loaded subjects like racism or ethnic tension, too often believers fall into the familiar ditches of denial or despair. Some people think that talking about racial reconciliation only makes things worse. They believe "everything's fine." There are others who are weary and feel hopeless. To borrow from Fannie Lou Hamer, a civil rights leader in the 1960s, they are "sick and tired of being sick and tired." But lament offers a way to vocalize frustration and sorrow that is not only helpful but also biblical. Lament provides a place to go with the pain of racism and prejudice. It's a prayer path for talking to God and to one another about the brokenness of the world.

Lament gives us a way to vocalize the complicated emotions connected to racial reconciliation.

Empathize with Others

Lament creates a language to "weep with those who weep." It helps us express sorrow with one another. Lament gives us a voice of empathy. It communicates that while we may not understand, we are willing to walk alongside a brother or sister in pain. Rather than immediately moving into fix-it mode, praying a lament prayer with a brother or sister grieving over a racial incident or an injustice helps you enter into his or her sadness or frustration.

Too often we are silent. I've made that mistake many times. Out of fear of saying the wrong thing or asking an unintentionally hurtful question, we don't say anything. And the silence is deafening. Whether in a personal meeting over coffee or a pastoral prayer during a Sunday service, I've seen the power of empathy that comes from prayers of lament.

Talking to God together communicates "I care."

Memorialize the Lessons

The book of Lamentations serves as a memorial—a way to mark a painful moment in the past with a view toward not forgetting the lessons. Laments help us remember. As we listen to these pain-filled prayers, we are reminded that history tends to repeat itself if we don't learn from the past.

The spirituals, as a form of lament, invite us to feel the trauma of the African American experience and ponder the implications. Although they aren't necessarily Christian prayers per se (some are), they are historical and cultural expressions of the pain and trauma of racial injustice.

African American spirituals serve as memorials.

Lament gives us a language to vocalize, empathize, and memorialize any kind of pain, but especially when it's associated with racial injustice. Regardless of your ethnicity, listening to the spirituals can be instructive. For majority-culture Christians, this chapter provides an opportunity to step outside our culture, demonstrate humility, and learn from this rich tradition. For minority Christians, this chapter could serve as an encouragement regarding the contributions of African American songwriters and theologians. You may also find yourself resonating with the unique pain and sorrow expressed in these historic, cultural laments.

The spirituals tune our hearts to the pain in our nation's history. They help us feel and understand the struggle under the horror of slavery and segregation. They show us the value of listening to lament.

Spirituals help us in the journey toward reconciliation.

The History of the Spirituals

The first slave ship arrived on the coast of North America on August 20, 1619, a year before the Pilgrims arrived on the Mayflower. A Dutch frigate docked a few miles south of Jamestown, Virginia, with twenty Africans.[2] Over the next three centuries, the trafficking of Africans over

---

2. Bruno Chenu, *The Trouble I've Seen: The Big Book of Negro Spirituals* (Valley Forge, PA: Judson, 2003), 7.

the Atlantic totaled more than ten million people.[3] An act of the US Congress banned the trans-Atlantic slave trade in 1808. However, over the next fifty years, slavery dramatically increased through "domestic slave trade" within the boundary of the United States. The number of slaves tripled until they constituted nearly a third of the southern population.[4]

While physical demands and horrific treatment marked the life of slaves, they also faced enormous challenges in the practice of their faith. Plantation owners often refused to allow slaves to gather for worship, fearing they might be emboldened to seek freedom. As a result, slaves met secretly. They would gather in "hush arbors"—covert worship services in the woods or swamps.[5] The singing at these gatherings often featured a "call and response" pattern, with a degree of improvisation and enthusiasm. Jemar Tisby writes, "The precariousness of their existence led Christian slaves to cry out to God with a passion and exuberance that has become characteristic of many black church traditions."[6] Their secret churches, sometimes called the "invisible institution," created a refuge from the dehumanizing conditions.

The spirituals emerged in this brutal context. They expressed emotions for both the individual and the entire community. Albert Raboteau puts it this way: "One person's sorrow or joy became everyone's through song. Singing the spirituals was therefore both an intensely personal and vividly communal experience in which an individual received consolation for sorrow and gained a heightening joy because his experience was shared."[7] Spirituals became the language of suffering and hope for those who lived in exile.

---

3. Jemar Tisby, *The Color of Compromise: The Truth about the American Church's Complicity in Racism* (Grand Rapids, MI: Zondervan, 2019), 29.

4. History.com editors, "Slavery in America," History (website), November 12, 2009, https://www.history.com/topics/black-history/slavery.

5. Tisby, *The Color of Compromise*, 52.

6. Tisby, *The Color of Compromise*, 52.

7. Albert J. Raboteau, *Slave Religion: The "Invisible Institution" in the Antebellum South* (Oxford: Oxford University Press, 2004), 246.

The abolition of slavery in 1863 did not silence the spirituals. These songs became the expression of African Americans living with segregation, burning crosses, Jim Crow laws, sharecropping, the Ku Klux Klan, and lynchings. The spirituals also played a unifying role in the civil rights movement of the 1950s and 1960s. Songs like "We Shall Overcome" have their roots in this rich tradition.

The spirituals provide a window into the history and the heartache of African Americans.

Spirituals as Cultural Lament

The spirituals are expressions of contemporary lament. While these sorrow songs were not biblically inspired, they are instructive. George Faithful, in his journal article titled "Recovering the Theology of the Negro Spirituals," says, "Few genres of song have been as significant historically, literarily, musically, and theologically as the 'Negro spiritual.' For their original singers, they were songs of praise, lamentation, and resistance."[8]

Every spiritual expresses a unique perspective on the hardship of slavery and segregation. Spirituals highlight the pain. One of the most heartfelt is "Sometimes I Feel Like a Motherless Child." It vocalizes the haunting loneliness of slavery. Bruno Chenu writes, "Because the separation of families was such a dramatic, though common, experience, the slave was an orphan with an unfathomable sadness of heart. The slave no longer had brothers, sisters, father, or mother."[9]

Sometimes I feel like a motherless child,
a long ways from home, a long ways from home.[10]

---

8. George Faithful, "Recovering the Theology of the Negro Spiritual," *Credo ut Intelligam*, December 13, 2007, https://theologyjournal.wordpress.com/2007/12/13/recovering-the-theology -of-the-negro-spirituals/.

9. Chenu, *The Trouble I've Seen*, 118.

10. "Sometimes I Feel Like a Motherless Child," Hymnary (website), accessed April 26, 2019, https://hymnary.org/text/sometimes_i_feel_like_a_motherless_child.

The hymnal of the Evangelical Covenant Church uses this spiritual as a responsive refrain to the reading of Psalm 88, a lament psalm that expresses a deep sense of abandonment:

> O Lord, God of my salvation,
>> I cry out day and night before you.
> Let my prayer come before you;
>> incline your ear to my cry!
>
> For my soul is full of troubles,
>> and my life draws near to Sheol.
> I am counted among those who go down to the pit;
>> I am a man who has no strength. (Ps. 88:1–4)

Lament psalms and the spirituals have parallel themes. Abandonment, loneliness, and a desperate need for God's help characterize portions of Psalms 12 and 94:

> Save, O Lord, for the godly one is gone;
>> for the faithful have vanished from among the children of
>>> man. (Ps. 12:1)
>
> Who rises up for me against the wicked?
>> Who stands up for me against evildoers?
> If the Lord had not been my help,
>> my soul would soon have lived in the land of silence. . . .
> When the cares of my heart are many,
>> your consolations cheer my soul. (Ps. 94:16–17, 19)

The spirituals provided suffering people with a personalized voice to strengthen their faith. They refused to hide the "repercussions of living through an unbearable drama," says Chenu.[11] One such song is "Master Going to Sell Us Tomorrow?" I've visited the location in Montgomery, Alabama, where slaves were auctioned. Today it's a fountain

---

11. Chenu, *The Trouble I've Seen*, 116.

at the center of a roundabout, a beautiful landmark that hides the depravity of the human trafficking in the past. But hear the words of this spiritual and feel the horror of people trafficked as property and family relationships viewed as disposable:

> Mother, is master going to sell us tomorrow?
> Yes, yes, yes!
> O, watch and pray!
>
> Going to sell us down in Georgia?
> Yes, yes, yes!
> O, watch and pray!
>
> Farewell, mother, I must lebe [leave] you,
> Yes, yes, yes!
> O, watch and pray!
>
> Mother, I'll meet you in Heaven.
> Yes, my child!
> O, watch and pray![12]

Stop and consider what you just read. Imagine the generational trauma of children ripped from parents' arms, husbands estranged from their wives, fathers isolated from sons, and mothers disconnected from daughters. Harriet Jacobs, an escaped slave, recounts one horrifying moment:

> On one of these sale days, I saw a mother lead seven children to the auction block. She knew that some of them would be taken from her; but they took all. The children were sold to a slave-trader, and their mother was bought by a man in her own town. Before night her children were all far away. She begged the trader to tell her where he intended to take them; this he refused to do. How could he, when he knew he would sell them, one by one, where he

---

12. Quoted in Chenu, *The Trouble I've Seen*, 114.

could command the highest price? I met that mother in the street, and her wild haggard face lives today in my mind. She wrung her hands in anguish, and exclaimed, "Gone! All gone! Why don't God kill me?" I had no words wherewith to comfort her. Instances like this were of a daily, yea, of hourly occurrence.[13]

The spirituals help us feel this trauma. They personalize suffering. As we listen, we can empathize in ways unknown before.

The spirituals, as a cultural lament, also sought to transform suffering. Identification with the sorrows of Christ and his physical mistreatment appeared in many songs. They envisioned a connection between the crucifixion of Jesus and the hangings, whippings, and other abuses that were a part of the African American experience.[14] The slaves saw Jesus not only as one who could empathize (Heb. 4:15) but also as one who was lynched. This intimate identification brought both sorrow and comfort—some of the key fruits of lament. The well-known spiritual "Were You There When They Crucified My Lord" features this somber tone:

Were you there when they crucified my Lord?
Were you there when they crucified my Lord?
Oh, sometimes it causes me to tremble, tremble, tremble.
Were you there when they crucified my Lord?[15]

This spiritual became a song of identification and hope. The suffering of Jesus connected with the experience of the slave. In the same way that certain psalms provide comfort as the historical context is brought into personal application, "Were You There" became deeply encouraging to slaves. As Arthur Jones explains, the song provided "hope that their present suffering was not the end of the story. Just as

---

13. Harriet Jacobs [Linda Brent, pseud.], *Incidents in the Life of a Slave Girl* (Fairford, UK: Echo Library Classics, 2011), 15.

14. Arthur C. Jones, *Wade in the Water: The Wisdom of the Spirituals* (New York: Orbis, 1993), 30.

15. Quoted in Chenu, *The Trouble I've Seen*, 201.

the Bible tells the story of Jesus who died to save humanity, so the suffering of the slave has meaning for life in the present and the future."[16] The spirituals point to Jesus as one who understands. These cultural laments were a deep well of comfort from the injustice in the world.

The spirituals continued their influence on the African American experience well beyond the days of slavery and segregation. These songs were the first expression of American modern music.[17] Their themes continued to live on through the civil rights movement. Probably the most famous reference to a spiritual was in the conclusion to Dr. Martin Luther King's "I Have a Dream" speech on the steps of the Lincoln Memorial on August 28, 1963:

> When we allow freedom to ring, and when we let it ring from every village and every hamlet, from every state and every city, we will be able to speed up that day when all God's children, black men and white men, Jews and Gentiles, Protestants and Catholics, will be able to join hands and sing in the words of the old Negro Spiritual: "Free at last. Free at last. Thank God Almighty, we're free at last."[18]

King leveraged a spiritual from the past to unify and inspire action in those attending the historic march. "Free at Last" is not unique in that power, Jones observes. "This message was carried into the air on the wings of hundreds of African American spirituals, continually transforming the lives of all of those who heard or sang them."[19]

Spirituals, like lament psalms, identify with pain while pointing people to hope.

Though these historic songs are not inspired, they are instructive. I hope this chapter helps you gain a new appreciation of the

---

16. Jones, *Wade in the Water*, 30.

17. Richard Newman, *Go Down, Moses: Celebrating the African-American Spiritual* (New York: Clarkson Potter, 1998), 9.

18. Martin Luther King, Jr., "'I Have a Dream,' Address Delivered at the March on Washington for Jobs and Freedom, August 28, 1963," Martin Luther King, Jr. Research and Education Institute, Stanford University, accessed April 26, 2019, https://kinginstitute.stanford.edu/king-papers/documents/i-have-dream-address-delivered-march-washington-jobs-and-freedom.

19. Jones, *Wade in the Water*, 136.

power and significance of the spirituals. Perhaps you'll be motivated to explore other songs in this rich tradition. In the same way we learn an elevated view of God by reading a Puritan prayer or singing "A Mighty Fortress," spirituals give us a glimpse into the soul of African American brothers and sisters trying to survive with unrelenting injustice and sorrow.

Four Ways Spirituals Help Us

Listening has been the goal of this chapter. Before we move to learning how lament helps us walk together, let me crystallize four ways I think the spirituals help us.

A Broader View of History

A major challenge in racial reconciliation is one's view of history. Textbooks and history classes tip toward whatever culture is dominant in your education, family, or hometown. As a result, we tend to have a more myopic view of the past than we realize.

The spirituals provide a window into the history of our country and African American Christianity that many of us (especially among the majority culture) need. As I've entered into conversations and researched African American history, I'm often alarmed with how little I know. I'm grieved it has taken me this long to realize this gap. The spirituals invite us to consider the experience of African American Christians. They bring the history of racial injustice to the surface. They give us a broader understanding of history.

Humble, Respectful Listening

Spirituals also help us practice James 1:19 ("quick to hear, slow to speak, slow to get angry") before we take additional steps in the conversation about racial reconciliation. Our minority brothers and sisters are often grieved by the lack of respect given to their culture and history.

How many people have you heard ask: "Why do we need black history month? What about white history month?" Too often majority-culture Christians fail to realize the lack of attention to the history, distinct challenges, and contributions of African Americans and other minorities.

While racial harmony requires humble, respectful listening from both sides, I think there is a greater responsibility on those of us in the majority culture to take the first step. Exploring the spirituals in this chapter may have been a good start for you. I would suggest there's a lot more to learn—not only about the spirituals but also in the entire discussion about racial harmony. Listening to the spirituals can build the maturity muscles for future conversations about much more challenging and controversial topics. But if you don't start practicing listening now, there's little hope it will appear in the future.

Honoring the Depth of Sorrow

I learned through my own sorrow and writing on lament that grieving people desperately need others to empathize with their pain. Too often we are guilty of moving quickly to solutions. Sometimes well-meaning people even take the hurtful role of "policing" others' pain, wondering out loud why they can't "move on."

The spirituals help us grapple with the pain of the past. They give us the opportunity to honor the depth of sorrow—even to enter into it. Songs have a way of speaking to the heart at a level that is very helpful. Like the psalms of lament, the spirituals have the potential to give us a new level of understanding without moving so quickly toward resolution. Cornel West comments:

> The spirituals not only reveal the underside of America—in all of its stark nakedness; they also disclosed the night side of the human condition—in all of its terror and horror. But they do so

through an unequivocal Christian lens. . . . We often leap to the religious consolation of the spirituals without lingering on sadness and melancholia.[20]

In other words, listening to the spirituals helps us understand the sorrow of the past and the present.

Personalizing Lament

The spirituals are the sound of a personalized cultural lament. Each chapter in this book concludes with a lament prayer so that you can see this illustrated. I want you to make the connection between the biblical language of lament and your own expression. The real power of lament for racial reconciliation emerges when we start to express our hurts, fears, frustrations, and sorrows through this historic prayer language. I've included some worksheets in appendix 2 to help you take your own steps. And the next chapter will explore this further. For now, I simply want you to see the power of making lament your own.

The spirituals personalize sorrow.

Hopefully, you can now understand why I reframed the question about lament in the context of the church. I'm sure every kind of church—both majority- and minority-culture—needs to grow in lament. But I think it's helpful to know that there is a significant difference in American church history related to lament. The experience of the African American church is marked by this sorrow song in ways that many of us might miss.

Understanding this gap, listening to minority brothers and sisters, and learning from them are vital parts of the racial-reconciliation process. Lament starts us on a journey to take some additional steps together.

Listening opens a door for us to walk together under the banner of Jesus.

---

20. Cornel West, "The Spirituals as Lyric Poetry," in *The Cornel West Reader* (New York: Basic Civitas, 1999), 464.

LAMENT PRAYER

Dear heavenly Father, when I think of the oppression of the past, humans you made owned by other humans you made, my soul cries out. It is deeply distressing. The anguish of my ancestors, the pain and sorrow that still lingers, it's all too deep for words.

O Lord, I am perplexed. I don't understand our history. Why must people be in shackles? Why the separation of brown and white people? How could your name and your word be used against those who love you, Lord?

Lord, deliver us from our sorrows, and comfort us in our affliction. Forgive those who sinned against your people. Bring about redemption and reconciliation—let your glory shine in our broken places. Answer us when we call, O Lord. Hear our cries for unity and peace. Accomplish what only you can by your power.

Even in my distress and confusion I know you are God—almighty, glorious, wonderful, trustworthy, righteous, everlasting, sovereign, and good. You are more than words can express. I will put my trust in you, O Lord. You are our Rock and our Redeemer. I rest my heart in you—the one who can carry all our burdens.

Trillia Newbell,
director of community outreach for
the Ethics and Religious Liberty Commission
of the Southern Baptist Convention,
Nashville, Tennessee

Discussion Questions

1. Prior to reading this chapter how would you have answered the question about whether the evangelical church understands lament? Would

you have differentiated between the histories of lament in white churches and in African American churches?

2. Describe the church culture in which you were raised. Did you have any experience with a culture that differed from the one in which you were raised?

3. Which of the five steps in the racial-reconciliation process are the most challenging for you? Why do you think that is?

4. What did you know about the spirituals prior to this chapter? What in particular did you learn?

5. Which spiritual was most meaningful to you? Why?

6. Review the four benefits of spirituals at the end of the chapter. Which of them are most applicable to you?

7. Rate your listening quotient. When it comes to the topic of racial reconciliation, what grade would you give yourself regarding listening and learning?

8. What action steps do you need to take in light of this chapter?

3

WALK

The Bridge of Lament

Father, while I know you love your people, I am confused as to
why the history of my ancestors is so painful and dark. Lord,
I'm calling on your name to enlighten me and allow me to see
this painful history through the lens of your gospel. Lord, even
in my pain and hurt I choose to love because you are love.

KIMBERLY WHARTON[1]

The evening of Dr. Martin Luther King Jr.'s assassination, the country
mourned and cities burned. Riots erupted in more than one hundred
communities, including the nation's capital.[2] The shock and anger
of the cold-blooded murder in Memphis lit a fuse of outrage. Unrest
swept the country.

---

1. Lament prayer by Kimberly Wharton, an African American member of College Park
Church, used by permission.
2. Michael Rosenwald, "That Stain of Bloodshed: After King's Assassination, RFK Calmed
an Angry Crowd with an Unforgettable Speech," *Washington Post*, April 4, 2018, https://www
.washingtonpost.com/news/retropolis/wp/2018/04/03/that-stain-of-bloodshed-after-kings
-assassination-rfk-calmed-an-angry-crowd-with-an-unforgettable-speech.

But not Indianapolis.

While there were small conflicts the night of King's assassination, Indianapolis was spared citywide rioting. Many historians believe the relative calm on April 4, 1968, should be credited to an impromptu, empathetic speech by Robert Kennedy in the heart of the city. Kennedy's presidential campaign planned an event in Indianapolis. When word of King's assassination reached the campaign staff and law enforcement, local leaders recommended canceling the event. News of riots around the country created a concern for Kennedy's safety.

Despite the risks, the senator from Massachusetts determined to give his speech. The campaign rally was in the middle of a predominately African American neighborhood.[3] The police could not offer sufficient protection. Robert Kennedy proceeded anyway. After mounting a makeshift platform, Kennedy delivered a six-minute address to a waiting crowd. His speech was not what they expected. "I have bad news for you, for all of our fellow citizens, and people who love peace all over the world, and that is that Martin Luther King was shot and killed tonight."[4] If you listen to the audio, you can hear the audience gasp and cry.

As his speech continued, Kennedy spoke with clarity and empathy:

> For those of you who are black and are tempted to be filled with hatred and distrust at the injustice of such an act, against all white people, I can only say that I feel in my own heart the same kind of feeling. I had a member of my family killed, but he was killed by a white man. But we have to make an effort in the United States, we have to make an effort to understand, to go beyond these rather difficult times. . . . What we need in the United States is not divi-

---

3. "The Speech," Kennedy King Memorial Initiative, accessed May 16, 2019, http://kennedy kingindy.org/thespeech.

4. Robert Kennedy, "Statement on Assassination of Martin Luther King, Jr., Indianapolis, Indiana—April 4, 1968," John F. Kennedy Presidential Library and Museum, accessed May 16, 2019, https://www.jfklibrary.org/learn/about-jfk/the-kennedy-family/robert-f-kennedy/robert -f-kennedy-speeches/statement-on-assassination-of-martin-luther-king-jr-indianapolis-indiana -april-4-1968.

sion; what we need in the United States is not hatred; what we need in the United States is not violence or lawlessness; but love and wisdom and compassion toward one another, and a feeling of justice toward those who still suffer within our country, whether they be white or they be black.[5]

Kennedy's heartfelt words on the fateful day of King's assassination became one of the most famous speeches of his short life. But it also was one of the most important moments in the history of Indianapolis.

Kennedy's empathy bridged a divide that filled other cities with chaos.

Landmark for Peace Memorial, Indianapolis

To mark the significance of Kennedy's speech, the city of Indianapolis created the Landmark for Peace Memorial at Seventeenth and Broadway—the location of the campaign rally. A winding path cuts through a green field and crests on a mound between the life-size images of King and Kennedy. The memorial makes it appear that both men are emerging from metal slabs opposite each other. The walkway passes between the figures. The two men reach toward each other. The path places you between the outstretched arms of King and Kennedy. A full copy of Kennedy's speech is posted a few feet away. It's a moving tribute to a dark day in our nation's history.

Unfortunately, few residents in Indianapolis know about the memorial or its history. That's one reason why I organized a trip for our church staff on Martin Luther King Day. We secured a large bus and over fifty of our staff traveled to this historic spot. On our journey, I shared the background behind the memorial, including part of Robert Kennedy's speech.

On a cold day in January with heavy snowflakes falling, we walked together along the winding path to the memorial. After pausing to quietly consider the powerful images of King and Kennedy, our church

---

5. Kennedy, "Statement on Assassination of Martin Luther King."

staff gathered in a circle. I read from Colossians 3—the vision that "Christ is all and in all"—and we prayed for greater unity, love, and diversity in our church. We asked God to make us more considerate of one another and for reconciliation in our church. It was a moving experience. There were tears and hugs, especially for the minority brothers and sisters who traveled with us.

One of our African American sisters, named Yolanda, walked with me back to the bus. As we followed the footprints on the snow-covered path, she opened up. Yolanda told me her father had been involved in the civil rights movement in Marks, Mississippi. Martin Luther King stayed in their home. I was stunned. She wasn't trying to impress me. The intimacy and tenderness of the visit to the memorial opened a door.

Yolanda and her husband, Keith, had joined our church about five years earlier. They graciously navigated the uncomfortable waters of being a minority in a mostly white suburban church. I had no idea about Yolanda's personal connection to the civil rights movement. I asked her to share her story with our staff.

Yolanda took the microphone on the bus. She described her life in Marks, Mississippi, sharing about her experience with a father who pastored a local church and served as a leader in the civil rights movement. She told our staff about Dr. King's visit to her home, as well as the Poor People's March and the Mule Train, an idea conceived when King visited Marks in March 1968.[6]

Yolanda's story was impactful.

I stood behind her as she shared. No one moved. Our staff marveled not only at what we were hearing but also that this story was coming from one of our own church members. Behind the Yolanda that we all knew was a beautiful and painful story—one she just allowed us to see.

---

6. Debbie Elliott, "How a Mule Train from Marks, Miss., Kicked Off MLK's Poor People Campaign," NPR (website), May 13, 2018, https://www.npr.org/2018/05/13/610097454/how-a -mule-train-from-marks-miss-kicked-off-mlks-poor-people-campaign.

Our pilgrimage to the memorial and our painful prayers opened a door for Yolanda to share.

At the conclusion of our visit, Yolanda pulled me aside. Sensing something powerful in the trip, she said, "Pastor Mark, wouldn't it be great to take a trip down south and see some of the other places related to the civil rights movement?" Apparently Yolanda could see what was obvious to me as well: something special had happened during this visit.

"Yolanda, we can do that. I'd love to. I'd need your help. Let's figure out how to make that happen."

Civil Rights Vision Trip

Nine months later, Yolanda and I traveled with fifty leaders of our church from a variety of ethnicities on a five-day Civil Rights Vision Trip. We wanted to replicate the experience, wondering what would happen if people from our church—both minority and majority believers—visited historic sites connected to the history of civil rights in the United States.

For years our church had offered global vision trips to catch a vision for unreached people groups. Vision trips shaped the global-mission culture of our church as people saw firsthand the opportunity and the needs around the world. I was hoping for the same impact with racial reconciliation.

I knew the trip would form new relationships between people from different ethnicities as they traveled together and processed their experience. I dreamed about putting into practice the model steps of loving, listening, lamenting, learning, and leveraging as we moved out of our comfort zones and into the lamentable history of race relations in our country.

The trip became a pilgrimage.

But not without risk.

At an orientation meeting before the trip, I could sense the tension in the room. There was a palpable excitement but also an obvious nervousness. As I explained the vision for the trip, I encouraged the participants to realize that this would be more than a history tour. The trip was going to be a deeply personal and even traumatic experience. We were going to see ugly things. But I also encouraged them that the gospel could transform the dark issues from the past with healing. I shared the vision of helping our church grow in our experience of biblical unity in diversity and racial reconciliation.

Our journey was designed to bring change.

It was important for the fifty leaders not only to share the same vision but also to speak the same language of lament. Therefore, I walked them through the four elements of lament (turning, complaining, asking, and trusting) with a worksheet to help them examine a lament psalm and write their own.

Our Pilgrimage

Our civil rights pilgrimage featured visits to Birmingham, Montgomery, Selma, Marks, and Memphis.[7] We toured the 16th Street Baptist Church, the site of an infamous church bombing in 1963 that killed four young black girls. We later learned one of the girls was a relative of a member of our church. In Montgomery, we visited the "Lynching Memorial," or the National Memorial for Peace and Justice. Over eight hundred large, rusted steel boxes are suspended from the ceiling, each representing a county in which at least one racial lynching took place.[8] The names of people and the dates on which they were lynched are etched into the metal. We visited the bus stop where Rosa Parks boarded the bus and took her stand against segregated seating.

---

7. For a full itinerary, see appendix 3.
8. "Memorial," EJI (The National Memorial for Peace and Justice website), accessed May 16, 2019, https://museumandmemorial.eji.org/memorial.

Others visited Dexter Avenue Baptist Church, the congregation pastored by Dr. Martin Luther King Jr. In Selma, we walked the Edmund Pettus Bridge—the site of the "Bloody Sunday March" on March 7, 1965. We stopped at a cotton field in full bloom, considering what the scene must have looked like a generation or two previously. While in Marks we visited with Yolanda's family and learned about the historically black colleges and universities (HBCUs). We also visited a memorial to Emmett Till, whose abduction and gruesome murder sparked new urgency in the fight for civil rights. Finally, we visited the Lorraine Motel, the location of King's 1968 assassination in Memphis.

Besides the historic sites and museums, a highlight was worshiping at a local Missionary Baptist Church. I'm not sure if this church, in the heart of the Mississippi Delta, had ever hosted so many white Christians. The tension was thick as the service began. The pastor spoke right into the issue: "Now folks, ya'll just need to relax. Some of you are worried that the IRS or the FBI showed up to church this morning. These friends are brothers and sisters in Christ, and we've come to worship together today." And with that, the service began. It proved to be a sweet day of worship followed by a fellowship meal together. By the time we loaded up in our bus, we had made new friends.

The Civil Rights Vision Trip was transformative. The history, images, sights, and sounds were deeply moving. Our white church members confronted the vast gaps in our understanding and empathy. Our minority brothers and sisters faced the trauma and history of the past, creating painful questions as they processed our trip. The visits produced a rawness among us—like a dam pent up with troubled water ready to break at any moment.

Lament Opened a Door

Every morning we started our day with a time of Bible study and sharing. We used a lament psalm as our guide. While we traveled to various locations, we used the lament worksheets and examined laments in the Bible.

Using the turn, complain, ask, and trust framework, we studied a psalm to discover where each of these elements appeared. We identified observations in the text and prepared to share. After a few minutes I walked up and down the aisle with a microphone, facilitating the examination of the lament psalm. I asked follow-up questions to help us dig into the text. It was a powerful time of group Bible study.

But then we personalized our study, writing our own laments.

Using the now-familiar pattern of turning, complaining, asking, and trusting, I gave our fellow travelers time to reflect on the previous day, what they were processing, and how they wanted to talk to God in prayer. In the same way that every psalm has a context, so their lament prayers were borne out of their painful experience the previous day.

The real power, however, was when we started to share our prayers.

I led us into a prayer posture, reminding us all that what we were about to hear was personal and sacred. And then individuals read their freshly written laments. Here is one:

Father and Lord, my hope is in you alone. Surely your eyes range throughout the earth to strongly support those whose hearts are yours. Although I believe this, it is hard to see it right now. And I struggle to know my role in what we call racial reconciliation. This task seems too big and complicated. Evil has been so pervasive and continues to be all around us towards my brothers and sisters, within us, within me. Have you abandoned your people, O God? Will you be an absentee landlord?

And then I see the cross. And I see your early church, so diverse and so beloved. And I remember that you are eternally good, powerful, and unchanging.

Move in us for your glory, O Lord! Move in our hearts, my heart, our church's ethos, [and] the whole church for your glory.[9]

Reading our prayers became sacred moments as we plumbed the depths of our sorrows and reaffirmed our confidence in God to help us. Tears came to the surface. Lament provided a common voice to vocalize our grief. It helped white brothers and sisters empathize.

Lament led to vulnerability.

Jesus, I don't understand the cruelty that I've seen. The depths of evil toward fellow humans—yet within my heart I know that, without you, my heart contains the same evil. How many times will I find that evil in my heart?

Please help me to understand my brothers' and sisters' pain. Help me to feel and know the horror of hatred. Help me not to deny the seeds of hatred in my heart. I trust you for you are good. You reveal the hidden heart. You reveal with love and for my good and your glory. Unite us together.[10]

Lament also led to hope. Our African American members took a great risk coming on the civil rights trip. Lament gave them a language to talk to God and the rest of us in confronting the trauma of racism.

In the midst of great sorrow, help my heart to be still in you. When the evil of racism visits me, forgive me for my unbelief that you are in control. When the thoughts of doubt, shame, and hate seem to be the place I run to, remind me of your endless well of compassion and grace. Above all, orient my heart to see you in all things.[11]

Studying a lament psalm, witnessing the candid and inspired honesty in the Bible, and then writing our own laments to the Lord made the morning devotionals a critical part of our pilgrimage.

But the conversations didn't end there.

9. Lament prayer by Lance Pfeiffer, used by permission.
10. Lament prayer by Lydia Abdnour, used by permission.
11. Lament prayer by Jay Justice, used by permission.

Walking Together

As the bus traveled the highway, God brought us together. Something remarkable happened.

After our devotional time and our prayers of lament, I asked for people to share their thoughts and experiences based upon the places we visited the previous day. We started by hearing from our African American brothers and sisters.

A few expressed their reservation at coming on the trip. They didn't want to confront the depths of pain in our nation's history. They worried if our white brothers and sisters would listen to them. Others shared perspectives on how hard it can be to attend our church as a minority. A few opened up with disturbing stories and experiences on Sundays: offensive jokes, inappropriate comments, and hurtful statements. It was hard to hear. An African American dad shared his deep fear at how his son might be treated by the extended family of a white girl he was interested in dating. Unfortunately, the experience of our African American church members was fairly consistent. They loved our church, but all of them had hurts. And now they were willing to talk about the pain.

But there was more.

We listened as they shared about other challenges in our culture. A dad wept as he told us about his fears with his son starting to drive on his own. He explained "the talk"—on what he called "DWB," driving while black. This dad gave his son specific instructions as to what he should do if pulled over. Other African American parents nodded their heads. The fear and pain were evident and widespread. One shared about an incident with a traffic stop. After the officer approached his vehicle, he asked for permission to secure his registration from the glove box. The officer obliged him but said, "I'm just going to draw my weapon and hold it by your head while you do that." Someone gasped. More heads nodded.

I wish these were the only painful stories. They weren't. The more sites we visited and the more we lamented, the more honesty we heard from our African American brothers and sisters.

Having a language to process our pain helped us confront the ugly remnants of insensitivity, injustice, and racism.

Lament also helped our white brothers and sisters. Many of us—myself included—struggled with how little we knew not only about the history of racial injustice but also about the current experience of our fellow church members and friends. I remember walking away from the "Lynching Memorial" and thinking, *Why didn't I know this history?* As we toured other museums, it was a common refrain from our white tour members. The information was painful. But the gaps in our understanding were shocking.

Our times of lament offered an opportunity to vocalize our grief and humbly seek the Lord's help. Our white brothers and sisters demonstrated humility and empathy as they talked to God about what they were learning and feeling. One member of the trip wrote:

> Reflection on visiting 16th Street Baptist Church, Birmingham Civil Rights Museum . . . and conversations with friends on the bus—Father I need you. We need you—as a nation and as a church! We need your direction and your strength. This division seems too big for us. The history is too hurtful. The present is painful. Hearing that our own brothers and sisters have felt pain in our own church body and felt at times it was or is not a safe place when the tension is high—is difficult, almost unbearable. Lord only you can change me. Act in me. Only you can unite us. . . . You can do this, Lord! You want us to be unified. You call us to love one another. My hope is in you only.[12]

Prayers like these started to endear us to one another. The walls of indifference and distrust started to fall. Awkward questions could be

---

12. Lament prayer by Heather Day, used by permission.

asked. New friendships developed. We cried a lot, but we laughed too. We experienced a rare level of sweet and honest connectivity. We were on a journey together—a pilgrimage of sorts.

Lament opened a door for us to walk together.

The vision for this book is to see believers in Jesus from different ethnicities united. So often our stated desires outpace the steps we take. In other words, when it comes to racial reconciliation, we might talk a good game. However, tangible steps feel elusive. I've heard many of my white brothers and sisters say, "What can I do?" Rather than quickly entering the typical fix-it mode of many white evangelicals, there's something powerful about weeping with those who weep.

A key to learning is lamenting.

The compassion of Robert Kennedy probably saved Indianapolis from a night of citywide turmoil. But I don't think we should view that event as unusual. Lamenting together breaks down barriers, unites hearts, and creates new bonds.

Lament is a helpful starting point. It can bridge the divide of mistrust and insensitivity. If we'll commit to loving one another, listening to each other, and lamenting together in the body of Christ, racial reconciliation can start to happen.

I've seen it.

◊

LAMENT PRAYER

Father in heaven, we know you are good in all you do and wise in all your ways. We dare not presume upon your providential purposes, and you do not owe us any answers or explanations. And yet we do not understand why you have allowed your church to fall into such sin and division.

How could the same churches that preached your love have turned around and hated their brothers? Why can we never seem to escape from the shadow of this evil? Are we doomed to repeat the sins of our fathers?

We who are one spiritual family, speaking the same language of salvation, still struggle to relate as children of the same Father. Sometimes we wonder if anything can be done, if the final sentence has already been rendered. But we ask that you would do more than we could ever ask or imagine, that you would work a miracle that can only be explained by the gospel of Jesus Christ.

Bring down the mighty from their thrones and exalt the humble. In a church that has often contented itself with worldly comfort, we ask that you would once again equip your servants with spiritual power to turn the world upside down. We—especially those of us who continue to perpetuate prejudice, knowingly or unknowingly—do not deserve your grace.

Still we plead upon the blood of Christ that your will would be done on earth as it is in heaven.

Collin Hansen,
editorial director of the Gospel Coalition,
Birmingham, Alabama

Discussion Questions

1. When it comes to the subject of race relations in the United States, how would you describe your knowledge of that history? Why do you think that is the case?

2. Describe the "tone" of conversations about racial reconciliation in your hometown, school, or church when you were growing up. What about now?

3. As you read this chapter, what particular sentences made you uncomfortable? Why do you think you felt that way?

4. Which lament prayer was most meaningful to you? Why?

5. Describe your conversations about race with people from other ethnicities. How do you think they could have been more impactful?

6. Have you experienced prejudice or mistreatment because of your ethnicity? Would you feel comfortable sharing with others what happened? Why or why not?

7. In your own words, why is lament uniquely helpful in setting up the conversation for racial reconciliation?

8. In what other ways could lament prayers be used for opening a door for racial-reconciliation conversations?

PART 2

LAMENT AND
MAJORITY CHRISTIANS

4

WEEP

The Healing Grace of Empathy

The Bible calls us to weep with those who weep; it doesn't
tell us to judge whether they should be weeping.

H. B. CHARLES JR.

The aim of this book is to discover how the biblical language of lament
opens a door for racial reconciliation. While lament is never enough
by itself, it helps.

In part 1, we've explored the meaning of lament, learned how the
spirituals help us listen, and considered the way lament empowers us
to walk together in reconciliation. In part 2 we'll explore how lament
assists those of us who are part of the racial majority. We'll learn the
way lament allows us to lead with empathy, encourages us to speak
when tempted to be silent, and expresses repentance when necessary.

I'm starting by addressing those of us who are "white" because I'm
trying to model a process for reconciliation—a commitment to love,

listen, lament, learn, and leverage. I think it's helpful and necessary for majority-culture Christians to intentionally lean into this subject and take the first step. Regardless of your ethnicity, I hope you will take the time to read each chapter.

Empathy Is Essential

There is hope for racial reconciliation as the church, especially white evangelicals, leads with empathy. We need to learn to "weep with those who weep."

A bedrock biblical truth is the empathetic nature of Jesus and the calling to follow his example. Centuries before the birth of Christ, the prophet Isaiah described the coming Messiah as "Immanuel" (Isa. 7:14), which means "God with us," and as a "man of sorrows and acquainted with grief" (Isa. 53:3).

In the New Testament we see this in full color. John says, "The Word became flesh and dwelt among us" (John 1:14). God loves the world by sending his Son (John 3:16). The incarnation makes a powerful statement. Jesus embraces our pain, suffering, and temptation (Heb. 2:11–12). He weeps at the tomb of Lazarus, feels compassion for the crowds, agonizes in the garden, grows weary from the press of ministry, and laments over the waywardness of the holy city Jerusalem. Jesus knows our brokenness. The empathy of Jesus invites us to pray with confidence (Heb. 4:15–16).

God doesn't redeem at a distance.

But that's just the beginning. Believers must follow the example of Jesus. Possessing the mind of Christ requires considering the needs of others as more important than our own (Phil. 2:3–5). When we bear one another's burdens, we fulfill the law of Christ (Gal. 6:2). A concern for one's neighbor, widows, and orphans expresses true obedience (Matt. 22:39; James 1:27).

No wonder the apostle Paul writes the following to the church in Rome: "Rejoice with those who rejoice, weep with those who weep.

Live in harmony with one another" (Rom. 12:15–16). This admonition was written to a diverse church. A concern for others is a vital expression of the gospel. Jason Meyer explains:

> The church is called to put the light of Christ in its prominent place on the nightstand of the nation. . . . Was racial hatred between Jew and Gentile hard in the first century? Yes. Was it too hard for the gospel? No. . . . What other religion has a God who cried and bled for his enemies? How, then, can Christians settle for knowing the suffering of others from a safe, intellectual distance? . . . In Christ, we can reflect to others the compassion we have received from him.[1]

A church can't be Christian without empathy. Empathy is essential to Christianity and racial reconciliation.

Empathy Defined

Before we go any further, let's define empathy. It's the ability or willingness to understand and care. In his book *Made for Friendship*, Drew Hunter says: "Empathy . . . is the ability to understand and adjust to someone's emotional state. It is the capacity to enter his mind, to peer out at the world through his eyes. . . . We understand how [others] feel and why they feel it. And we also feel it with them."[2] Empathy enters into the sorrow of another person's experience. Mika Edmondson writes:

> Empathy means that we take the burdens, the sorrows, the concerns of our neighbors upon ourselves to the point of crying tears with them. . . . We think about their children as if they were our children. We think about their concerns as if they were our personal concerns, and we cry tears with them.[3]

1. Jason Meyer, "How the Gospel Turns Racial Apathy into Empathy," The Gospel Coalition, July 15, 2016, https://www.thegospelcoalition.org/article/how-gospel-turns-racial-apathy-into-empathy/.
2. Drew Hunter, *Made for Friendship: The Relationship That Halves Our Sorrows and Doubles Our Joys* (Wheaton, IL: Crossway, 2018), 89.
3. Mika Edmondson, "Hopeful Strategies for Hard Conversations," The Gospel Coalition, April 5, 2019, https://www.thegospelcoalition.org/conference_media/hopeful-strategies-hard-conversations/.

We empathize not because we fully understand but because we have been freely loved by Christ. Entering the pain of another and lamenting with others demonstrates the heart of Christianity. This is especially true when it comes to the painful fruits of racism and ethnic division. Choosing an empathetic posture will not always be comfortable. It involves walking into messy and complicated pain. Misunderstanding or missteps may happen. But our perseverance to "weep with those who weep" should be rooted in the gospel.

The spiritual beneficiaries of the incarnation should be the emotional benefactors of those in pain.

Lament as Empathy

Lament talks to God about our sorrow out of a desire for him to understand. That's one reason why we love the Psalms, especially laments. They express what we feel as we wrestle with the effects of a broken world. Laments give voice to feelings of abandonment, confusion, hurt, and other strong emotions.

Lament is the prayer language of empathy.

Listen to these examples:

Why do you hide your face?
    Why do you forget our affliction and oppression?
For our soul is bowed down to the dust;
    our belly clings to the ground. (Ps. 44:24–25)

O Lord, how long shall the wicked,
    how long shall the wicked exult?
They pour out their arrogant words;
    all the evildoers boast.
They crush your people, O Lord,
    and afflict your heritage. (Ps. 94:3–5)

I could list many more. Lament psalms help us know we are not alone in our struggle. They normalize our battle with pain. They remind us that God welcomes our messy worship. He understands. Why else would he inspire over a third of the Psalms with this empathy-rich prayer language?

Perhaps you can remember a helpful friend who sat beside you in a dark moment of sorrow and simply said: "I'm so sorry. Let me pray for you." Beyond any words, the step of prayerful communion brought this friend into your sorrow as you looked to the One who truly understands and has the power to help.

Empathetic lament creates a community.

Lament and Racial Empathy

Let's take this a step further. Consider what it would look like if white brothers and sisters prioritized lamenting for minority Christians. What if lament prayers expressed our solidarity even when we don't fully understand? Imagine pastoral prayers or a brief lament on social media designed to communicate that we are weeping with those who weep. What if we led with lament even if we are not sure why some are weeping or even if they *should* be weeping? There's something attractive here. Again, Jason Meyer is helpful: "Do you see the beauty in the unity of a multiethnic church mourning together? Black inner-city mothers who fear their children may not make it home at night should be able to weep on the shoulders of those who don't look like them—those who join their tears instead of judge them."[4]

When it comes to racial reconciliation, weeping with those who weep needs to be our first step. Lament can be a helpful, biblical language because empathy is uniquely Christian.

An Empathy Test

Part of the challenge with empathy is our blindness to its absence. Our backgrounds, experiences, media outlets, and culture shape a narrative

---

4. Meyer, "How the Gospel Turns Racial Apathy into Empathy."

that can be empathy-lite. Sometimes we even find creative ways to justify our lack of concern. Every once in a while it's good to examine ourselves.

We tend to overestimate our competency in compassion.

In a sermon on racial harmony, I tested my congregation's empathy by sharing part of a lecture given by Mika Edmondson, an African American pastor from Grand Rapids, Michigan. I'd like to challenge you to take the same test.[5]

Dr. Edmondson delivered a lecture titled "Is Black Lives Matter the Next Civil Rights Movement" to the Council of the Gospel Coalition. After providing a thorough and careful examination of the strengths and weaknesses of Black Lives Matter and its differences from the civil rights movement, Edmondson issued a passionate, pastoral plea:

> My wife has to beg me (a grown 37-year-old man) not to go out to Walmart at night, not because she's afraid of the criminal element, but because she's afraid of the police element. Because she knows that when the police see me, they aren't going to see Mika Edmondson, pastor of New City Fellowship Presbyterian church. When they see me, they aren't going to see Mika Edmondson, PhD in systematic theology. When they see me, all they're going to see is a black man out late at night. And she knows we're getting stopped at 10-times the rate of everybody else, arrested at 26-times the rate of everybody else, and killed at 5-times the rate of everybody else. Black Lives Matter can see the injustice in those statistics. How can Black Lives Matter see the value of a black life better than we can? Why does Black Lives Matter care more about the value of my life than you do?[6]

I then asked our congregation some questions. I'm inviting you to answer them as well.

---

5. I'm thankful to Jason Meyer for this idea from his sermon "Trusting God in the Darkest Night," July 10, 2016, https://bethlehem.church/sermon/trusting-god-in-the-darkest-night/.

6. Mika Edmondson, "Is Black Lives Matter the New Civil Rights Movement?," The Gospel Coalition, June 24, 2016, https://www.thegospelcoalition.org/article/is-black-lives-matter-the-new-civil-rights-movement/.

When you read this quote, where did your heart go first? Did you gravitate toward the statistics? Did you think, *Where did he get those?* Did you hear his reference to Black Lives Matter and begin to offer your argument about that movement? Did you hear his comment about being afraid of the police and think *that's ridiculous?*

Or were you able to weep with an African American pastor whose wife is afraid for him to visit Walmart at night because of how he might be perceived? Does our brother's statement cause you to want to understand him and hear why he feels that way? Or do you immediately want to argue with him? While curiosity about statistics may be a habit of thoughtful people, do you find yourself minimizing the concern of the pastor and his wife? Is their concern also *your* concern for them? Discussions about statistics, social movements like Black Lives Matter, or policing aren't off the table. But part of the problem is that we often come to the topic of race without empathy. And that's not just a racial problem. That's a human problem.

For many in my mostly white church, the quote and questions revealed a knee-jerk, emotional reaction. The example surfaced a bias toward arguing and self-justification—not empathy. As one white brother told me: "You nailed me. I was arguing, not weeping in my mind."

I've been there. Maybe you are too.

The chasm between the majority and the minority church is wide—even if people attend the same congregation. While there are many reasons for this cultural fissure, one significant cause has been the lack of empathy on the part of white Christians. We've turned a blind eye to our nation's history, the church's role in maintaining the status quo, and our minority brothers' experience. With the advent of social media, their painful stories are receiving more attention— and validation. But without empathy on the part of the church, the divide will deepen.

One way to grow as majority Christians is realizing that empathy—weeping with those who weep—should be our first step.

Leading with Empathy through Lament

The title of this book suggests there is hope for racial reconciliation if we lament together. How can majority Christians communicate compassion through the hurts, fears, and frustrations experienced by their minority brothers and sisters? Let me try to put some handles on the connection between lament and empathy in three areas.

Personally

Lament tunes our hearts to be more inclined toward empathy. By practicing lament personally, you raise your sensitivity to the pain of others. This is especially true when it comes to racial reconciliation. Out of love, we have to listen—and then lament the pain we hear.

Lament pulls the pain close.

Consider a few practical steps. Perhaps you could start by reading one of the lament psalms more frequently. By reading these minor-key songs, you'll become more aware of the lingering sorrow in the world. Next, as you watch the news or flip through social media, don't allow the struggles and sorrows of minorities to remain at a distance. Take time to lament. Talk to God about what you see. Lament the brokenness of racial division. Push against the normalization of racial tension. Immerse yourself in the pain of your minority brothers and sisters by lamenting. It's transformative.

Dietrich Bonhoeffer (1906–1945) was a German pastor executed by the Nazis near the end of World War II. His books *The Cost of Discipleship* and *Life Together* are still widely read and quoted. But prior to Bonhoeffer's fame and his resistance to the Nazis, his life was shaped by a year in Harlem with the Abyssinian Baptist Church, an African American congregation.

In 1931 Bonhoeffer immersed himself in the African American community. He studied the history of slavery and segregation, read leading minority writers, listened to spirituals, and served in the community. Reggie Williams writes, "By practicing empathy in Harlem, he opened himself to exploring and revising the way he saw the world from within a community that was foreign to him."[7]

Upon his return to Germany, Bonhoeffer used the lessons from Harlem to shape his teaching and pastoral ministry. He invited students on retreats, discussing theology and listening to his collection of African American spirituals.[8] Bonhoeffer's empathetic immersion led him to consider the plight of Jews under Nazi rule. He said, "Only he who cries out for the Jews can sing the Gregorian chant."[9] Bonhoeffer's year in Harlem informed his opposition to the Nazis. His immersion in the African American community laid the foundation for much of his poignant writing.

Empathetic lament will change you.

Relationally

As we come to see the value of lament, we can also allow it to help us care for our minority brothers and sisters. We can fulfill Paul's command to "weep with those who weep" by taking active steps to communicate our awareness of their pain. We can commit to walking with them. In the same way lament psalms give voice to what we are feeling, a prayer of lament with a black or Latino brother or sister after a racially charged incident could create a new level of solidarity.

Imagine what it could mean to minority Christians for you to acknowledge a troubling event on the news or recognize the mistreatment

---

7. Reggie Williams, *Bonhoeffer's Black Jesus: Harlem Renaissance Theology and an Ethic of Resistance* (Waco, TX: Baylor University Press, 2014), 79.

8. Williams, *Bonhoeffer's Black Jesus*, 113.

9. Williams, *Bonhoeffer's Black Jesus*, 102, quoting Bonhoeffer, in Eberhard Bethge, *Dietrich Bohoeffer: A Biography*, rev. ed. (Minneapolis: Fortress, 2000), 441.

they've experienced personally. Consider the bridge that could be built if you led with "Sister, my heart is grieving over what I'm seeing right now. I don't understand everything that's going on. But I'm asking the Lord to help us walk together." Perhaps you'd even take another step and ask: "How are you doing? How can I pray for you?" This kind of lament is powerful. Says Daniel Hill:

> It sees suffering not as a problem to be solved but as a condition to be mourned. . . .
>
> Lament gives us resources to sit in the tension of suffering and pain . . . to acknowledge the limitations of human strength and to look solely to the power of God instead.[10]

When I've applied lament in this way, it has often opened a door. I say "often" because sometimes I haven't built enough relational capital. At other times, a minority brother or sister has not been ready to open a deeply painful area of his or her life. But it's still worth the effort. I've witnessed lament creating a tender moment or an opportunity to learn as a minority brother or sister shares at a deeper level. Sometimes what I hear creates more questions. At other times, I don't know how to process—or even whether I agree—with what is shared with me. But I still need to listen. I don't like the tension when I find another painful layer in the conversation about racial harmony. The only hope for progress is to start with a commitment to "weep with those who weep."

Racial reconciliation is possible only in the context of relationships. That starts by knowing minority Christians, sharing meals, "doing life" together, and also embracing their hurts and struggles. As I've gone deeper relationally, I've discovered there is far more pain under the surface than what I imagined. My brothers and sisters have many painful stories, but you need to have relational credibility before they'll

---

10. Daniel Hill, *White Awake: An Honest Look at What It Means to Be White* (Downers Grove, IL: InterVarsity Press, 2017), 111–12.

share. The personal nature of the pain and years of rejection create a deep-seated caution about being open and sharing their pain. That's another reason why the chasm between the white and black church gets wider and deeper.

Empathetic lament can help us overcome this relational blockade.

Prayerfully consider giving this a try. The next time a racial incident hits the news or a powerful movie premiers on the subject of race, or maybe in response to this book, evaluate your empathy level. Do you feel sadness for minority brothers and sisters? Or are you unbothered or unaffected? Empathy awareness is helpful. And then consider reaching out to one or two minority friends. Ask about their perspective. Acknowledge your need to learn. Share your grief with them. Ask if they would join you in a prayer of lament.

It won't solve everything. But lamenting together is a great place to start.

Publicly

Another way we can embrace the power of lament is through our public prayers. This is one reason why I've invited Christian leaders to write prayers of lament for this book. I want you to hear what it might sound like in a public venue. The cause of racial reconciliation would be greatly helped if white evangelicals publicly joined our minority brothers in their sorrow.

For example, before each sermon in a series on racial harmony, I led with a lament prayer. Here's one example:

How long, O Lord, will division or defensiveness mark your people? The legacy of racism has cut a deep wound that still affects even our approach to this Sunday. Some come apprehensive. Others come annoyed. Still more come hurting. Others come confused. O God, the layers in our culture, our history, and our hearts are so complicated.

Jesus, we need you. We believe that you want us to be one. We believe that the world will know that we are your disciples by our love for one another. We believe that you gave your life to ransom a people from every tribe, nation, and tongue. We believe that you want your church to be united. And we confess that the brokenness is so deep, our defensiveness so quick, and our solutions so few that talking about racial reconciliation is complicated and scary.

Lord, help us to be quick to hear, slow to speak, and slow to become angry. We need the Holy Spirit to teach us, guide us, and heal us. We trust that your grace is brighter than the darkness of our past, more glorious than the pain we've experienced, and deeper than any wound. And so, in our brokenness we say, "The steadfast love of the Lord never ceases." Amen.

I dream of white evangelical churches engaging in a process of reconciliation with corporate laments. This kind of prayer allows church leaders not only to end their silence but also to acknowledge the pain and struggle our minority brothers and sisters feel. Rather than denying the pain or faking our way through it, lament prayers create a place for the healing to begin.

Laments communicate that the church cares.

"Weep with those who weep" is a command. It expresses the heart of the gospel. It is how Jesus treats us. Daniel Hill explains:

When our sisters and brothers of color are suffering—or worse, being killed—it's an absolute imperative that we suffer alongside them. We need to show them that we see them and that we see their suffering. We need to show them that we see the injustice behind the suffering and that we lament its ongoing presence. We need to be locked arm in arm with our extended family, crying out to God in a collective spirit of lament.[11]

---

11. Hill, *White Awake*, 116.

Empathy is an essential aspect of Christianity. It communicates compassion. But it also calls us to action.

In Montgomery, Alabama, there is a historical marker identifying where Rosa Parks boarded the bus and refused to give up her seat. A few blocks away is the Juliette Hampton Morgan Memorial Library. Few people know that years before Parks was arrested, Juliette Morgan (1914–1957), a librarian and the only child of a wealthy white southern family, spoke out and took action against racism in her city.

Morgan regularly confronted bus drivers over their unfair treatment of African Americans. At the time, blacks were required to pay their fare at the front door but were allowed to enter only through the rear. When a driver began to pull away, leaving a black woman behind, Juliette pulled the emergency cord and castigated the driver.[12] This was not the first or the last time she would intervene.

Juliette wrote multiple letters to the local newspaper, *The Montgomery Advertiser*, against the injustices of segregation and the poll tax.[13] For nearly a decade, Juliette Morgan spoke up. But it was costly. She was targeted by various white supremacy groups and received threatening phone calls. Someone burned a cross in her front yard. Tragically, the relentless opposition led her to take her life.

One of the driving forces behind Morgan's boldness was her participation in an interracial prayer group called the Fellowship of the Concerned. Since no white church would risk holding an integrated prayer meeting, the fellowship met in black churches. The impact of lamenting in this prayer meeting was profound. Edmondson comments: "After participating in this prayer group, Juliette Hampton Morgan began to see the injustice of segregation for what it was. She began to see that it was out of step with the Christian faith, that it was out of step with the anointing of Christ."[14]

---

12. Edmondson, "Hopeful Strategies for Hard Conversations."
13. "Juliette Hampton Morgan, 1914–1957," Civil Rights Digital Library, accessed July 17, 2019, http://crdl.usg.edu/people/m/morgan_juliette_hampton_1914_1957/.
14. Edmondson, "Hopeful Strategies for Hard Conversations."

Weeping with those who weep emulates the heart of Jesus. It builds a bridge of grace over the chasm of division and injustice. It provides comfort to those who are hurting.

Empathy isn't the only step, but it should be the first one.

◊

LAMENT PRAYER

How long, O Lord? How long will your body be divided? How long will the stronghold of racial prejudice and injustice be raised up defiantly against the knowledge of God? How long will your blood-bought bride keep building up the dividing wall of racial hostility you tore down? What will it take, Lord? How long must we wait for the gift of repentance to change the church from the inside out?

Look upon your church and see how she is plagued with both racial apathy and racial hostility. Why is empathy so rare and apathy so common among us? Instead of weeping with those who weep, we are quick to judge the tears and slow to join them. We are too quick to become angry and argue and too slow to see our biases and confess our blindness.

O Lord, move among us and move in us. We need a mighty rushing wind to blow away the poisoned air of prejudice. By the power of the Holy Spirit, turn our apathy into empathy and our hostility into unity. Break our hearts for our nation's shameful sin of slavery. Give us grace to come to grips with our history of hate and oppression and segregation.

O God of sovereign grace, change our hearts so that the next chapter of the church's story will read like reconciliation, not segregation. May the world know that we are Christians by our love. May your reconciled children not tolerate each other as different but love each other as family. May the love of Christ compel us with fresh grace to love one another genuinely, stand up for one another boldly, and weep with one another tenderly.

In the mighty name of Jesus, we pray.

Amen.

Jason Meyer,
pastor of Bethlehem Baptist Church,
Minneapolis, Minnesota

Discussion Questions

1. In your own words, how would you define *empathy*? How has your definition changed after reading this chapter?

2. Why is empathy essential to Christianity?

3. When you read Mika Edmondson's description of his wife's fears for him, and the reasons why, what was your reaction? What do you think the reaction would be from your friends or family?

4. How have the Psalms or other parts of the Bible provided comfort for you? What lessons are there for you when considering the racial-reconciliation conversation?

5. What step can you take personally to be more empathetic when it comes to the topic of race?

6. Why are relationships with minority Christians so critical to this conversation?

7. Consider a racial incident in the recent past, and write out a lament prayer reflecting on it.

8. In what "public spaces" do you think it would be helpful for white Christians to lament? What cautions, fears, or concerns do you have?

5

SPEAK

Ending the Painful Silence

You have seen, O LORD; be not silent!
O Lord, be not far from me!
PSALM 35:22

When it comes to racial injustice, the historical silence of most white Christians has been deafening.

For reconciliation to happen, we have to acknowledge that the problem is *not* that we've talked about racial reconciliation too much. We've not expressed our love, taken time to listen, embraced the language of lament, or put ourselves in a position to learn from our minority brothers and sisters. Additionally, we've not sufficiently leveraged the authority of the church to bring change. If we're honest, too often white evangelicals are known for retreating from the conversation—sometimes even spiritualizing disengagement. It's part of the reason for the deep division that still exists in the church.

This silence is destructive.

"Letter from Birmingham Jail"

Dr. Martin Luther King Jr. knew the discouraging indifference of the white church during the civil rights movement. With a few exceptions, the perspective on Dr. King within white evangelicalism generally ranged from tepid to hostile, deepening the divide between black and white churches.

Nowhere is the problem of silence more clearly addressed than in the "Letter from Birmingham Jail." The letter is one of the most important documents King penned. Besides providing a moral justification for the nonviolent protests in Birmingham, King directly addressed the silence of white church leaders.

On April 12, 1963, King was arrested for violating Alabama's law forbidding public demonstrations. He spent several days in the Birmingham jail. After his arrest, the *Birmingham News* published an op-ed piece written by eight pastors. They criticized King's tactics and called for patience. From the jail cell, King responded with his now famous letter. He took silence to task:

> We have to repent in this generation not merely for the vitriolic words and actions of the bad people, but the appalling silence of the good people. We must come to see that human progress never rolls on the wheels of inevitability. It comes through the tireless efforts and persistent work of men and women willing to be co-workers with God.[1]

King not only believed that the civil rights movement faced direct opposition from people motivated by racism. He also was weary of the silence from good people.

Dr. King pleaded for a united, forceful voice. He called the church to express its sorrow through a modern-day psalm leading to change.

---

1. Martin Luther King, Jr., "Letter from a Birmingham Jail—April 16, 1963," Martin Luther King, Jr. Research and Education Institute, Stanford University, accessed June 14, 2019, http://okra.stanford.edu/transcription/document_images/undecided/630416-019.pdf.

"Now is the time to make real the promise of democracy and transform our pending national elegy into a creative psalm of brother/sisterhood. Now is the time to lift our national policy from the quicksand of racial injustice to the solid rock of human dignity."[2]

Although King doesn't use the term *lament*, it certainly fits. Lament is how people talk to God and one another when pain or indifference tempts them to be silent. Lament is not the only language for speaking out. Sermons, books, individual conversations, op-ed pieces, and blog posts are all vital. But the premise of this book is that lament can be one way to open a door for reconciliation instead of indifference, fear, or ignorance.

Lament could be a way to end our silence.

Six Reasons Why We Choose Silence

Why has silence so often characterized white Christians when it comes to racial harmony? This is an issue I've had to work through. I'm still wrestling with when to speak, what to say, and how to express myself wisely and boldly. As I've taken a look in the mirror and talked to majority and minority Christians, there are several reasons why I think Christians choose silence. I'm going to unpack six areas to consider. My list is certainly not comprehensive. It would be helpful for you to reflect on other areas as well.

Fear

As I've talked to white Christians, it seems fear creates a lot of our silence. Some are afraid of saying the wrong thing. They don't want to hurt a minority brother or sister. Many worry about being misunderstood by people on either side of the racial-reconciliation divide. Others fear being labeled a theological liberal, a social justice warrior, or a cultural Marxist. There's also a fear of opening a "Pandora's box,"

---

2. King, "Letter from a Birmingham Jail."

or confronting either historical or personal bias. I could go on, but you get the point. Within white evangelicalism, fear intimidates us into retreating from the conversation.

Fear holds us hostage to silence.

Uncertainty

Another reason why we choose silence is uncertainty over facts and feelings. The topic of race is not only loaded but also complicated. When a racial incident hits the news or explodes on social media, people take sides. Even before all the facts emerge, opinions surface and conclusions are drawn. I've found myself confused by the information or bewildered by the divergent views in our culture and within Christian circles. I'm not sure what happened. I don't know what to say. I don't know what's appropriate. Faced with this fog of confusion, silence is the default.

Caution in speaking, which might be wise in one setting, morphs into a default pattern of prolonged silence.

Wounds

I imagine that some of you reading this book have wounds from trying to engage in the conversation. Perhaps you asked a well-intentioned question only to be shamed or rebuked. Maybe someone accused you of being racist. Or perhaps a family member made a conversation painfully awkward by an over-the-top response to something you said. It seems that whenever we engage on the subject of race, misunderstanding tends to follow. I've experienced this from both my majority and minority brothers and sisters. I've battled the thought *I'm not opening my mouth ever again.* You may have experienced prejudice yourself—even as part of the majority culture. And perhaps it's led to frustration about racial reconciliation.

Wounds from the past tempt us to be silent.

Ignorance

For many white Christians, we simply do not understand the layered issues of injustice and racism. Some people are unintentionally blind. Others choose not to learn more. As a result, we approach the subject of racial reconciliation without the wisdom of personal experience or sufficient background. Often our circle of friends isn't wide or deep enough to hear the painful stories of our minority brothers and sisters. What's more, our knowledge of history is usually limited to the perspective in which we were raised. One reason for the Civil Rights Vision Trip was to help our mostly white church grow in its understanding of both the history of the country and the experience of our minority brothers and sisters. Traveling together to these historic sites closed some of the unhelpful gaps.

Ignorance creates silence.

Selfishness

Let's get a bit more personal. We need to acknowledge that silence can be the product of self-centeredness. Sometimes we arrogantly assume we see an issue correctly. Perhaps we make the mistake of listening only to people who agree with us. Some people don't engage in the topic of race because it's too loaded, exhausting, and emotional. It's too hard. They avoid talking about racial issues because they're controversial and troubling. Silence is easier. It feels safe. I've also encountered people who think talking about racism makes the issue worse—a common refrain from some white Christians. Unfortunately, sometimes we ignore the topic because that's more comfortable.

Silence can be the fruit of selfishness.

Racism

Finally, I have to acknowledge that some people remain silent because they harbor racist ideas. They don't speak out because they believe or feel that minorities are inferior. They think white culture or white people are superior. It might not be stated that clearly. It usually isn't. Racism usually hides behind innuendo, statistics, broad-brush generalities, family bias, and personal hostility. But, for some, it's there.

Silence can become a passive weapon of superiority.

———

When you look at this list, with which category do you resonate? What is your reason for remaining silent? When a racially charged incident breaks, what tips you toward not engaging? We all have a gravitational pull to one of these justifications. And it would be helpful to assess our posture—and then take steps to change.

The Message of Silence

While we wrestle with that, let me emphasize a critical point and one impetus for my writing this book. The reasons behind the silence of majority, white Christians are not clear to our minority brothers and sisters. They wonder which issue creates the silence. Is my pastor ignorant? Is my small group leader fearful? Or are there even more grievous issues underneath? As I've engaged my minority church members, I've learned that silence on the part of the church is not just deafening; it's deeply hurtful. It raises legitimate questions that are painful and loaded. This is the trap the enemy has laid for us. It's why the discussion about race is so hard. And it's why change is so slow.

Silence is part of the problem.

It's taken me a while to understand the confusing message of silence. In one of our church forums on racial reconciliation, I vividly remember a minority brother sharing the tension he felt coming to church. He wondered why we were silent during a series of racially charged incidents that dominated the news. He found himself internally pleading, *Say something . . . please say something.* Our silence sent confusing and hurtful messages. Minority church members left wondering why we were silent. I'm sure they battled not going too far in assigning motives. They tried to believe the best despite our silence.

This is not merely a problem on Sundays. It damages close relationships as well. During a meeting in my small group, a minority brother made a pointed and painful observation: "A month ago, I asked all of you what you thought about the diversity discussion at our church. None of you have answered. I'm struggling with not being hurt over your lack of response." A tense and honest conversation followed that only served to illustrate the painful problem of silence. Our minority brother desperately wanted to know if we were walking with him. What were his white brothers and sisters thinking? Did we really care? We certainly did. As we processed the conflict, it became evident that most of our white brothers and sisters didn't know what to say. Others had questions that they didn't know how to ask. They were afraid— really fearful—of saying the wrong thing. No one wanted to send a hurtful message.

But the silence itself was deeply hurtful.

One Solution to Silence: Lament

I've spent most of this chapter laying out the problem of silence. I think understanding the negative message of silence is a significant step forward for those of us in the majority culture. But we also need a language to help us when the pull of silence is strong.

This is where lament helps us.

Lament is the prayer language when God's people encounter the brokenness of the world. It's the biblical way to express sorrow when we don't know what to say. Lament vocalizes concern when life is hard and uncertain. This minor-key prayer keeps us talking to God and one another when pain and fear invade our lives. Instead of allowing silence to deepen the divisions, we can join together in lament.

Lament is a starting point that breaks through our silence.

How Lament Helps

As I've studied and written about lament, parallels have emerged between helping grieving people and racial reconciliation. It has become clear to me that lament can be helpful in the loaded conversations or the temptation toward silence. Whether the lament is expressed directly to God, to a friend at a coffee shop, to a living-room small group, or to a congregation during a pastoral prayer on Sunday, it can be a starting point.

How does turning to God in prayer, laying out our complaints, asking boldly, and choosing to trust help us navigate this silence-laden terrain? Let me suggest three ways.

It Acknowledges the Brokenness of the World

Pain births lament. It deals honestly with the real world. Lament candidly identifies the brokenness around us and in us. It acknowledges the gap between God's design for the world and our experience. Lament is the way the Bible talks about life in a sinful world.

> Give ear to my words, O LORD;
>> consider my groaning.
> Give attention to the sound of my cry,
>> my King and my God,
>> for to you do I pray.
> O LORD, in the morning you hear my voice;
>> in the morning I prepare a sacrifice for you and watch.
>
> For you are not a God who delights in wickedness;
>> evil may not dwell with you.
> The boastful shall not stand before your eyes;
>> you hate all evildoers. (Ps. 5:1–5)

Lament can be used to pray about the challenges of living in a world marked by the brokenness of racial division. Our prayers can acknowledge the presence of injustice. We can mourn the reality of misunderstanding.

Lament gives us a unified voice to grieve together over a broken world.

It Refuses to Remain Silent

Lament breaks through painful silence. It is how the psalmist prayed as he struggled talking to God. It's how to pray when God feels far away. Lament is the voice of grief when we're tempted to remain silent. It helps when we don't know what to say.

> In the day of my trouble I seek the Lord;
>> in the night my hand is stretched out without wearying;
>> my soul refuses to be comforted.
> When I remember God, I moan;
>> when I meditate, my spirit faints.   *Selah*
>
> You hold my eyelids open;
>> I am so troubled that I cannot speak. (Ps. 77:2–4)

What's more, when the psalmist struggles with injustice, he prays through the pain:

> Be not silent, O God of my praise!
> For wicked and deceitful mouths are opened against me,
>> speaking against me with lying tongues. (Ps. 109:1–2)

Even while the facts are unclear and emotions run high, lamenting the presence of racial tension is better than silence. We can acknowledge the hurt our minority brothers and sisters feel.

Lament refuses to allow silence to rule our lives.

It Seeks God's Help

In order for a prayer to be a lament, it must move through pain to a re-commitment of trust in God. In this way, lament provides a life-giving and unifying language for the church. While we may not understand all the complexities of racism and injustice, every Christian should be able to affirm that we need God's help. We should be able to cry out together for God's grace when misunderstanding, hurt, fear, prejudice, and injustice invade our relationships, especially within the body of Christ. Laments protest against the brokenness of the world by seeking God's help. They refuse to allow the effects of sin to create a state of resignation.

Laments keep looking to God.

> O my God, I cry by day, but you do not answer,
> and by night, but I find no rest.

> Yet you are holy,
> enthroned on the praises of Israel.
> In you our fathers trusted;
> they trusted, and you delivered them.
> To you they cried and were rescued;
> in you they trusted and were not put to shame. (Ps. 22:2–5)

When we are overwhelmed or battling fear, laments call upon God to come to our aid. They invite us to ask for God's deliverance.

> Consider how many are my foes,
> and with what violent hatred they hate me.
> Oh, guard my soul, and deliver me!
> Let me not be put to shame, for I take refuge in you.
> (Ps. 25:19–20)

Laments appeal to God while pain and confusion are in the air. They give us an opportunity to reaffirm our desire for unity and reconciliation. While we might not even agree on all the facts, we can seek the God of all grace to help us love one another. While solutions are complicated or unclear, lament could acknowledge our collective need for God's intervention. Surely we can all agree on that! A lament could be a way to express our sorrow and reaffirm our trust.

Laments are not the only solution. But they're better than silence.

Silence More Than Hurtful

Hopefully, this chapter has helped you realize the problem of silence when it comes to racial reconciliation. If you are a white evangelical, let me encourage you to consider not only how you might be tempted to be silent, but also where you could take a first step toward lament. I know it's complicated. There are risks. However, our historic silence deepens the divide in the church. It's part of the problem.

The enemy uses silence to create more pain and deepen the divide.

Additionally, our silence hinders change. If white Christians fail to acknowledge the issues of racial tension or injustice, cultural norms become further solidified. From the jail cell in Birmingham, Martin Luther King leveled this rebuke:

> So often the contemporary church is a weak, ineffectual voice with an uncertain sound. So often it is an arch defender of the status quo. Far from being disturbed by the presence of the church, the power structure of the average community is consoled by the church's silent—and often even vocal—sanction of things as they are.[3]

Silence isn't merely hurtful; it can be complicit.

Lament could be the strong, effective voice with a biblical sound. It could break the stronghold of the status quo. The church, especially white evangelicals, could be a prophetic voice, leading the way forward and building a bridge that spans the historic divide.

---

3. King, "Letter from a Birmingham Jail."

As we end our silence through lament, we'll start to end the cycle of misunderstanding and distrust. And we'll help our minority brothers and sisters know we care.

Lament ends our silence and opens a door for reconciliation.

⬦

LAMENT PRAYER

How long, sovereign and gracious Lord, will your people remain silent when we should speak? Will we remain passive when we should act? How long, sovereign and gracious Lord, will we allow fear, confusion, wounds, ignorance, selfishness, and racism to handcuff us from being the church of King Jesus in a world desperate for authenticity, empathy, healing, love, understanding, and reconciliation? How long, O sovereign and gracious Lord, until your churches on earth begin to reflect your church in heaven?

Kind and loving Father, give us hearts to love others as you have loved us. Enable us to truly be a 1 Corinthians 13 people so that all people will know that we are your disciples by the way we love one another (John 13:35), and by the way we love our neighbors as ourselves (Matt. 22:39). Help us to walk in the Spirit and bear the fruit of the Spirit, denying the desires of the flesh (Gal. 5:16–23) that dishonor you and disgrace your gospel.

Precious Savior, we are confident that the good work you have begun in us you will complete. We are certain of your promise that you will perfectly conform us to the image of yourself for your glory and our good (Rom. 8:28). As you do your supernatural work in us, make it evident and visible to others so that it will be impossible to deny the truth of your word. Fill us with yourself. Send us out as salt to purify and heal, and light to reveal truth and dispel darkness. This is why you came. May this be true of us as we go!

Danny Akin,
president of Southeastern Baptist Seminary,
Wake Forest, North Carolina

Discussion Questions

1. Prior to reading this chapter, what was your familiarity with the "Letter from Birmingham Jail"? What reaction did you have when you read portions of it?

2. Why is it important to start this conversation about race with majority Christians? What are the advantages and disadvantages of this approach?

3. In your own words, what is meant by each of the six reasons for silence listed below?

Fear
Uncertainty
Wounds
Ignorance
Selfishness
Racism

4. Which one is most tempting to you? Why do you think this is the case?

5. Reflect on the confusing message of silence. Can you think of a time in your life—unrelated to the topic of race—where people's silence was hurtful?

6. In your own words, how does lament help us to end our silence?

7. In what venues could you imagine using lament? What other applications come to mind?

8. Consider writing out your own prayer of lament over the problem of silence.

6

REPENT

Remembering with Remorse

We lament and repudiate historic acts of evil such as
slavery from which we continue to reap a bitter harvest,
and we recognize that the racism which yet plagues
our culture today is inextricably tied to the past.

"RESOLUTION ON RACIAL RECONCILIATION,"
SOUTHERN BAPTIST CONVENTION[1]

A personal lament on our Civil Rights Vision Trip created a powerful moment of reconciliation. It began with the tear-filled honesty of a white church member: "This is my story. I grew up in the South. Racism was a part of my culture—my family and my school. I laughed at jokes. Made racist remarks. I even carried small clubs in the back of my car we called 'nigger beaters.' I was *that* kid. What we are seeing on this trip is my story."

---

1. Adopted on the 150th anniversary of the Southern Baptist Convention, Atlanta, 1995.

His voice quivered under the brokenness. He paused.

An African American woman placed her hand on his shoulder. You could hear the muted sounds of crying as we traveled down the road. A few rows back, a minority brother said, "I forgive you." Another shouted, "We love you, brother!"

Repentance led to reconciliation.

A day earlier we visited the National Memorial for Peace and Justice—the "Lynching Memorial." Recall that eight hundred metal boxes, one for each county where at least one racial lynching took place, are suspended in the air with names and dates identifying confirmed lynchings. Walking among the boxes, I noticed a small huddle of people. A young white woman from our church wiped tears off her cheek. Pointing to one metal box, she said, "This is where I'm from." In front of the small huddle were dates and names telling of the people lynched from her hometown: Robert Williams—11.04.1881, Ira Johnson—07.15.1895, Tom Keith—08.16.1899, George Green—11.16.1933. I watched as people—both white and minority believers—consoled her.

Remorse opened the door for healing.

Both stories reflect the sorrow over sin. Both people lamented. One lamented his own sin. The other lamented the sin of her hometown.

Should they both be called "repentance"? Yes and No.

Should they both be called "lament"? Yes.

Repentance, Remorse, and Lament

In this chapter we'll consider the connection between repentance, remorse, and lament. All are essential in racial reconciliation.

Repentance is the change of mind, heart, and will that involves confession of specific sin and a change in our affections. Remorse is the heartfelt response when the weight of sin is understood (2 Cor. 7:10). Lament ties repentance and remorse together. It vocalizes deep sorrow for past wrongs, especially our own.

If you surveyed lament psalms, you'd find multiple examples of sorrow over one's own sin. Psalms 32 and 51 are helpful examples:

I acknowledged my sin to you,
    and I did not cover my iniquity;
I said, "I will confess my transgressions to the LORD,"
    and you forgave the iniquity of my sin. (Ps. 32:5)

Wash me thoroughly from my iniquity,
    and cleanse me from my sin!

For I know my transgressions,
    and my sin is ever before me. (Ps. 51:2–3)

Repentance turns from sin. Remorse is the emotion. Lament is the expression.

However, personal repentance isn't the only kind of lament. There can also be corporate repentance. This lament vocalizes sorrow over sin in a family, a city, a nation, or the culture. It joins in the collective expression of grief over sin—in the past and the present. This is where things get complicated.

While we can't technically repent of sins committed by other people, that doesn't mean we shouldn't honestly mourn the failures of the past. We can lament historical and societal sins, especially when the roots bear poisonous fruit today. We'll explore corporate remorse later in the chapter (p. 118). At this point, I'm merely establishing the legitimacy of mourning when the sins of the past continue to bear consequences. An example is our response to abortion. Mourning the sin of abortion is required not just for those guilty of ending a baby's life or failing to stop *Roe v. Wade* in 1973. We too should lament the loss of innocent lives. Moreover, we as a whole—a nation and a people—can confess and lament our national sins. Still further, for any ongoing tolerance of this infant genocide, we must acknowledge personal culpability and express remorse.

The Bible records examples of corporate remorse. Jeremiah, Nehemiah, and Daniel vocalized sorrow for the sins of the people. The prophet Jeremiah penned the book of Lamentations, the longest lament in the Bible. It mourns the judgment of God upon the city of Jerusalem. Jeremiah never wavered in his faithfulness, but he still identified with the sinfulness of the city:

> Let us test and examine our ways,
>   and return to the LORD!
> Let us lift up our hearts and hands
>   to God in heaven:
> "We have transgressed and rebelled,
>   and you have not forgiven." (Lam. 3:40–42)

Nehemiah offers a similar prayer:

> Let your ear be attentive and your eyes open, to hear the prayer of your servant that I now pray before you day and night for the people of Israel your servants, confessing the sins of the people of Israel, which we have sinned against you. Even I and my father's house have sinned. (Neh. 1:6)

Daniel's lament expresses the same sentiment:

> We have sinned and done wrong and acted wickedly and rebelled, turning aside from your commandments and rules. We have not listened to your servants the prophets, who spoke in your name to our kings, our princes, and our fathers, and to all the people of the land. . . . All Israel has transgressed your law and turned aside, refusing to obey your voice. And the curse and oath that are written in the Law of Moses the servant of God have been poured out upon us, because we have sinned against him. (Dan. 9:5–6, 11)

Some might try to limit corporate remorse to the Old Testament. But in Peter's sermon at Pentecost, he charged the entire crowd with crucifying Jesus (Acts 2:36). Paul rebuked the whole church at Corinth for pride in failing to deal with an issue of immorality (1 Cor. 5:3–6). Jesus called upon the church at Ephesus to repent from abandoning their first love (Rev. 2:5). Surely there were Jews who didn't participate in Jesus's crucifixion. There were probably people at Corinth expressing concern about the immorality issue. How else would Paul have heard about it? And the church at Ephesus likely had people who were still passionate about Jesus despite the tepid spiritual temperature.

My point here is not to reduce individual and corporate repentance to mean the same thing. Rather, it is to acknowledge that both are real even though they are different. While we can't personally repent of the sins of others, we certainly can express remorse for the sinfulness of the world in which we live, a world that is, in some sense, our world. We can be honest about the past. We can lament the extent to which we have contributed to and been a part of a culture that allows, sanctions, or benefits from the sinful actions of others—both past and present. And we can work to bring change.

Laments help us confess when we've sinned or been complicit. They allow us to express remorse and change our thinking and our behavior.

Laments give us a language for repentance and remorse. Let's get more specific as it relates to racial issues.

Personal Repentance

When it comes to racial reconciliation, to what extent should Christians, especially white Christians, repent or feel remorse? Let's start with what is obvious.

Where we have been guilty of personal sins, we should wholeheartedly lament and repent. There is no excuse for devaluing the image of God in our thoughts, words, or actions.

Let me give you a list of sins from which we might need to repent. I hope you'll take time for personal inventory—even considering other sins not listed here.

Racism

As I shared in chapter 1, when a group of people considers itself to be superior and discriminates based upon race, that's racism. This ideology infected the social fabric of American culture and continues to have implications today. "White" was considered superior. And there are still people who believe or feel that they are better than minorities. Racism lurks in their thoughts. It shows on their faces when encountering someone of a different ethnicity. It hides behind inappropriate jokes and quiet snickers. Racism devalues the image of God imprinted on every human being.

Racism is based upon a belief in your own superiority.

Let me be transparent. As I've learned more about racism, I've had to take a close look in the mirror—to examine feelings of superiority I didn't realize were there. For example, I took Latin as my foreign language instead of Spanish while in high school. Looking back, I lament the times I felt superior. I'm ashamed I said to my friends that Latin is the language of the scholar while using an ethnic slur to talk about Spanish. My friends laughed. I thought learning a dead language was better. And, honestly, I thought I was superior because of it.

But now I know I was really just being racist. It's awful.

Prejudice

Another sin we need to consider is the sweeping, unfair, and negative generalizations we make about people, especially minorities, but also women, the poor, the police, and other common targets. Prejudice takes our experience with one person or a group of people and projects negative qualities on everyone who is of a similar demographic. Racial prejudice makes assumptions about education, marital status, intelligence, work ethic, family makeup, morality, income level, spirituality, attitudes, crime rates, and other areas simply based upon something as incidental as the color of a person's skin. Prejudice creates a judgmental spirit as we paint with a sinfully wide brush. It mishandles statistics. It elevates personal experience as ultimate.

Prejudice justifies its conclusions before considering the unfairness of the charge.

Willful Ignorance

The third area for personal repentance is the intentional refusal to consider the history or circumstances connected to racial issues. As I've engaged in racial reconciliation, it's been shocking to me how many people in majority culture refuse to engage in reading or dialogue. Some justify disengagement with the charge that talking about racial issues is divisive. Others limit their information to particular news outlets, podcasts, or websites with an ideological slant. At other times, people avoid venues that might challenge their thinking. For example, when I preached a three-week series on racial reconciliation, I was disappointed to learn that some people went to other churches for the entire series. It wasn't many but enough to grieve me.

Intentional ignorance is sinful.

Defensiveness

One of the biggest hinderances to reconciliation is a defensive unwillingness to listen. In order to understand the experiences of our minority brothers and sisters, and what they are saying, white Christians may need to repent of a deep-seated guardedness when talking about race. I wonder how many conversations about reconciliation have imploded because someone said, "Are you calling me racist?" The opportunity for dialogue vanishes with the charge, "You're not going to make me feel guilty because I'm white." Now, I'm not suggesting the word *racist* is never overused. Nor am I advocating that people feel guilty simply because of the light pigmentation of their skin. I'm merely saying that it's surprising to me how quickly white Christians become defensive and how often the pain of minority Christians is met with emotional resistance. Christians believe in depravity and know the deceitfulness of the human heart. Therefore, we should have a humble posture and a teachable spirit. Sadly, this is often not the case.

We should be the first to repent of our defensiveness.

Pride

Another sin to consider is the prideful assumption that you would have listened or taken action if you lived in a previous generation. It's easy to look back at slavery, segregation, and the church's complicity with racism with an arrogant belief you would not have been involved if you lived during that time. Jesus took the Pharisees to task for this very issue:

> Woe to you, scribes and Pharisees, hypocrites! For you build the tombs of the prophets and decorate the monuments of the righteous, saying, "If we had lived in the days of our fathers, we would not have taken part with them in shedding the blood of the prophets." Thus you witness against yourselves that you are sons of those who murdered the prophets. (Matt. 23:29–31)

It's easy to build monuments to the past and act as if you would not have participated. Russell Moore applies Matthew 23 to the modern Christian response to Martin Luther King Jr.:

> [Jesus says] the problem is that you come and you decorate the tombs of the prophets. . . . And yet the reason that you are so comfortably able to honor them is because they cannot speak to you any longer. You honor them because they don't disrupt the power that you have or the social order that you have. . . . Martin Luther King is relatively non-controversial in American life, because Martin Luther King has not been speaking for 50 years. It is easy to

look backward and to say "if I had been there I would have listened to Dr. King,"—even though I do not listen to what is happening around me in my own community, in my own neighborhood, in my own church.[2]

We need to feel the weight of Jesus's rebuke. We might need to repent, as well. If we won't listen now, it's arrogant to think we would have listened in the past.

Inaction

The final sin is neglecting to take action. Lament calls us to do more than pray. It creates the right posture so that we can live out true repentance—reflecting a change in how we think and what we do. Unfortunately, many white evangelicals have a long way to go in this arena, myself included. For some reason we treat racial issues differently than other areas of social concern when it comes to action.

Let me use abortion as an example again.[3] Most evangelical Christians would affirm three truths: (1) we should never commit an abortion; (2) we should believe abortion is morally wrong; and (3) we should work to remove abortion from our culture. Our belief in the sinfulness of abortion leads to activism against it. In other words, it's not enough to be a Christian who is nonabortive (1). We need to be antiabortion (3).

Strangely, we don't typically apply the reasoning to racism. Many of us believe it's enough not to commit acts of racism (1) or not to think of people as inferior (2). We know racism is sinful. Most Christians are nonracists (2). However, not enough Christians are anti-racist (3). We don't take the same posture with the sin of

---

2. Russell Moore, "King and Kingdom: Racial Justice and the Uneasy Conscience of American Christianity," Russell Moore (blog), April 10, 2018, https://www.russellmoore.com/2018/04/10/king-and-kingdom-racial-justice-and-the-uneasy-conscience-of-american-christianity/.

3. The following example is taken from my notes at a lecture delivered by Jemar Tisby, "How We Get Free: Faith in the Black Freedom Struggle," University of Indianapolis, February 13, 2019.

racism as we do with the sin of abortion. We need to be anti-racist and take actions to confront racism, prejudice, and injustice where they exist.

We might need to repent of our inaction.

————

My list of personal sins to lament is not designed to be exhaustive. I'm sure there are more transgressions for us to confess and mourn. Perhaps this list will start you on the path of greater vulnerability and honesty as it relates to lamenting your sin issues. Reconciliation is possible only when we are honest about ourselves and where we've been wrong.

But lamenting our sins is only part of the solution.

Corporate Remorse

Underneath the surface of our personal sins is the complicated question of how to respond to the sins of the past, especially when they still bear toxic fruit today. On the one hand some (typically in the majority culture) wonder why they should be held accountable for events, policies, and laws from a previous generation. You might hear someone say: "I didn't own slaves. I wasn't alive during segregation. I didn't live in the South. How can I repent of something I didn't do?" That's a legitimate question. Some might see the conversation about corporate repentance as a slippery slope toward liberal theology, cultural Marxism, or the weaponizing of victimization. Do you feel the tension?

On the other hand, our minority brothers and sisters grieve over the unwillingness of many white Christians to fully acknowledge the horror of slavery, segregation, and racism in our nation's history and its generational impact even today. They wonder why white evangelicals rally against the cultural blight of abortion while failing to denounce white supremacy. Our minority brothers and sisters grow weary of the gaps in our nation's conscience and the selective history white evangelicals tend to celebrate.

While I think it's technically true that we can't repent of someone else's sins, we can certainly lament them. By embracing the language of remorse, we can make progress in the following ways.[4]

Acknowledge Historical Sins

We can start by being honest and transparent about the sins of the past. Sam Storms, in "Is It Possible to Repent for the Sins of Others?," suggests that we should "acknowledge that our ancestors and our contemporaries with whom we are in some manner connected or related, have transgressed the law of God."[5] We should humbly confess our knowledge about these historic sins, especially when the actions of the past are still bearing poisonous fruit today.

The Southern Baptist Convention (SBC) began in 1845 amid a controversy over whether slave-owning missionaries qualified for service. Matthew Hall writes: "Our own denomination was birthed out of a commitment to preserve and defend slavery. We cannot evade that historical fact."[6] The SBC was not alone. Other denominations have the same history. For generations the same groups that sang "Blest Be the Tie That Binds" were some of the staunchest proponents of white supremacy and the harshest critics of the civil rights movement.[7]

---

4. I'm thankful to Sam Storms and James Bruce for the ideas that led to these categories. See Sam Storms, "Is It Possible to Repent for the Sins of Others?," November 23, 2015, Sam Storms, Enjoying God (blog), https://www.samstorms.com/enjoying-god-blog/post/is-it-possible -to-repent-for-the-sins-of-others, and James Bruce, "Should We Apologize for Sins We Did Not Commit?," The Gospel Coalition, July 14, 2016, https://www.thegospelcoalition.org/article /should-we-apologize-for-sins-we-did-not-commit/.

5. Storms, "Is It Possible to Repent for the Sins of Others?"

6. Matthew Hall, "The Historical Causes of the Stain of Racism in the Southern Baptist Convention," in *Removing the Stain of Racism from the Southern Baptist Convention: Diverse African American and White Perspectives*, ed. Jarvis J. Williams and Kevin M. Jones (Nashville: B&H, 2017), 9.

7. Hall, "The Historical Causes of the Stain of Racism," 10.

That's why the SBC's resolution in 1995, the 150th Anniversary of the denomination, was an important step. It candidly acknowledged the sins of the past:

> WHEREAS, Our relationship to African-Americans has been hindered from the beginning by the role that slavery played in the formation of the Southern Baptist Convention; and
>
> WHEREAS, Many of our Southern Baptist forbears defended the right to own slaves, and either participated in, supported, or acquiesced in the particularly inhumane nature of American slavery; and
>
> WHEREAS, In later years Southern Baptists failed, in many cases, to support, and in some cases opposed, legitimate initiatives to secure the civil rights of African-Americans; and
>
> WHEREAS, Racism has led to discrimination, oppression, injustice, and violence, both in the Civil War and throughout the history of our nation; and
>
> WHEREAS, Racism has divided the body of Christ and Southern Baptists in particular, and separated us from our African-American brothers and sisters . . . [8]

I hope you find it hard to stop reading there. Remorsefully acknowledging the sins of the past is a helpful step toward reconciliation.

Disavow the Sins of Our Ancestors

The second step of corporate remorse can be to repudiate the sins committed. Says Storms, "We make it clear by confession and behavior that we want no part in that sort of wicked behavior."[9] Disavowing the past makes a powerful statement—one that might need to be regularly reaffirmed. James Bruce, reflecting on the Presbyterian Church of

---

8. "Resolution on Racial Reconciliation on the 150th Anniversary of the Southern Baptist Convention, Atlanta, Georgia—1995," Southern Baptist Convention (website), http://www.sbc.net/resolutions/899/resolution-on-racial-reconciliation-on-the-150th-anniversary-of-the-southern-baptist-convention.

9. Storms, "Is It Possible to Repent for the Sins of Others?"

America's resolution on racial reconciliation in 2016, calls this a "kind of repentance" in which we say, "That's not who we are. It's who we were, but it's not who we are now."[10]

By lamenting historical transgressions, we memorialize the error so that we do not forget the lessons of history. It goes beyond mere acknowledgment by joining in the remorse and repudiating the sinfulness of the past. One part of the 1995 SBC resolution is particularly instructive:

> Be it . . . RESOLVED, That we lament and repudiate historic acts of evil such as slavery from which we continue to reap a bitter harvest, and we recognize that the racism which yet plagues our culture today is inextricably tied to the past.[11]

This is a good start. But there are more steps to be taken.

Recognize the Patterns from the Past

Laments allow us to connect with the errors of the past and provide a present-day warning. The book of Lamentations was written for this purpose. It remembers and instructs.

Lamenting historical issues helps us to recognize the patterns in thinking, attitudes, and behaviors that are still with us today. We can use the past as a mirror for self and societal reflection. We can acknowledge the remnants of "the futile ways inherited from our forefathers" (1 Pet. 1:18). A call for remorse and repentance in this generation involves turning from any sin that has continued into our generation.[12] In the midst of a controversy about the issue of corporate culpability, Thabiti Anyabwile offered this helpful plea:

> I don't need all white people to feel guilty about the 1950's and 60's—especially those who weren't even alive. But I do need all of

---

10. Bruce, "Should We Apologize for Sins We Did Not Commit?"
11. "Resolution on Racial Reconciliation."
12. Thabiti Anyabwile, "He Said, She Said," The Gospel Coalition, April 12, 2018, https://www.thegospelcoalition.org/blogs/thabiti-anyabwile/he-said-she-said/.

us to suspect that sin isn't done working its way through society. I do need all my neighbors—especially from my brothers and sisters in Christ—to recognize that no sin has ever been eliminated from the world and certainly not eliminated simply with the passage of time and a willingness of some people to act as if it was never there.[13]

While we can't repent of other people's sins, we can certainly repent when ways of thinking and talking, customs, and broken systems still plague our lives today.

Work to Bring Change

Corporate laments are designed to create change in both our thinking and our actions. As we express remorse for the sins of the past, we should "put on" the new behaviors that fit with repentance. We can start by engaging more often in the conversation about racial reconciliation and committing to an anti-racist posture. We should actively seek reconciliation and restoration. We should pursue relationships with minority brothers and sisters. Churches can be intentional with diversity in their outreach and staffing. And we might consider what kind of generosity should characterize our lives in light of the sins of the past.

Repentance and Remorse Are Essential

Repentance is central to the gospel. Remorse is the heart-language of a people who know not only their sin but also what it cost their Savior. Beyond all the discussion about whether we can repent of sins of the past and what kind of sins we should confess, it's important for those of us who are white Christians to take some steps in this area.

Whether expressing sorrow over sins you've committed or the sins of your family, city, county, or nation, lament provides a way to respond. Where racially oriented sins characterize our lives, the biblical language of sorrow mourns the egregious actions that grieve God's

---

13. Anyabwile, "He Said, She Said."

heart and create division. And when we face the sinfulness of the past or the lingering effects of racism or prejudice in our culture, lament gives us a prayer language that speaks honestly and with compassion.

For too long we who are majority culture Christians have not sufficiently grieved over our own sins. Nor have we expressed enough sorrow related to the history of our country and the church when it comes to racial injustice.

Our problem is not that we've mourned too much.

I'm not interested in false guilt or token statements of sympathy. But without an honest acknowledgment of either our guilt or the sinfulness of the past, true unity will never happen. Repentance and remorse are essential.

Lament empowers Christians to express sorrow over sin so reconciliation can begin.

LAMENT PRAYER

O Lord, shouldn't it be easier for your people to love each other? Jesus bled to make us one, yet our oneness often feels untrue. How long will we mute the suffering of our sisters and brothers? How long will we echo Cain's slight, "Am I my brother's keeper?" Why, oh why, do we remain content with callousness rather than cultivate compassion?

While we cannot repent of others' sins, we also must not ignore our own. Rather than bear others' burdens, we blame them for having burdens. We would rather ignore evil that does not harm us than help those who are being harmed. We are selective with the sins we grieve over. We gloss over attitudes, assumptions, and prejudices that grieve you. Far too often we have been unlike Jesus. He entered into others' pain, yet we flee from it.

Bitterness blinds us from seeing. Hardened hearts hinder us from hearing. We justify our ignorance and excuse our bitterness. The effects of our sin on the fellowship of your people are devastating. Trust is broken. Love is stifled. Hope is darkened. Perseverance is wearied.

The gates of hell seem too strong at times. Yet Jesus promised that they shall not prevail. He promised to build his church—and he never lies. So, Lord, build your church. Where there is sin, expose it. Where we are blind, enlighten us. Where there is prejudice, purge it. Give us eyes to see people as you do. Help us grieve over what grieves you. And above all, lift our eyes to Jesus, the author and finisher of our faith, who shed his blood to forgive our sins and unify us as one people.

We are needy. He is able. Help us, Lord, we pray. Amen.

Garrett Kell,
lead pastor of Del Ray Baptist Church,
Alexandria, Virginia

Discussion Questions

1. In your own words, how would you define *repentance* and *remorse*?

2. To what extent and in what situations do you think corporate repentance or remorse is appropriate? Do you think the 1995 resolution from the SBC was necessary? Why or why not?

3. Review the list of personal sin issues. Which ones do you see in your own life? How has your perspective changed since reading this book?

4. Review the four categories of corporate remorse. Which is the easiest for you to embrace? Which is the most challenging? Why?

5. What does it mean to be antiabortion? What would it look like to be anti-racist? Give practical examples.

6. What are some troubling questions with which you are wrestling right now? What issues or topics do you need to study and consider?

7. Take some time to write out a personal lament over your sins against people of other races or ethnicities. Do the same for corporate sins. Share your lament with a friend. Consider sharing it with a minority believer and asking for his or her feedback.

PART 3

LAMENT AND MINORITY
CHRISTIANS

7

PROTEST

The Voice of Exiles

Lament is an act of protest as the lamenter
is allowed to express indignation and even
outrage about the experience of suffering.

SOONG-CHAN RAH

A meeting at McDonald's fueled racial reconciliation at our church.

Two African American brothers attended our mostly white church for several years. They came from different backgrounds and for unique spiritual reasons. However, as we would later learn, their experience was not easy. While many people welcomed them, they also encountered strange looks or cautious greetings. At other times, they were ignored or treated suspiciously. They endured insensitive comments and questions. Some of their kids were exposed to racially inappropriate humor.

Sundays were hard.

Our church believes in our spiritual oneness in Christ (Col. 3:11) and in our collective bearing of God's image (Gen. 1:27). Yet, as these minority brothers listened to the same sermons, sang the same songs, and shared in the Lord's Supper, they often felt a profound sense of "otherness."

Sunday should have felt like home. But their church experience was more like an exile.

Some of my majority-culture brothers and sisters might be thinking, *Wait. Sundays are hard for lots of people. Why single out their experience?* I'm sure my minority brothers and sisters have heard this kind of response. And it hurts—deeply. You see, it's one thing for a member of the majority to feel lonely, struggle with relationships, or experience isolation regarding taste in music or some other issue. But it's another thing to feel "other" when both history and society tend to reinforce that painful isolation. And it's hurtful when church isn't a refuge from the sense of racial inferiority.[1]

Unfortunately, the tension for the minority church members continued beyond Sunday when some of their minority friends questioned their motives for attending a suburban, mostly white church. Family members asked hurtful questions. Others made assumptions. Some accused them of abandoning their history.

They experienced alienation from both sides.

And yet they persevered.

After they chose to make our church their home, the twice-a-month meetings at McDonald's started. They met with one of our pastors to talk about racial reconciliation in the church, share their experience, seek his counsel, and pray together. Over Egg McMuffins and thin pancakes, they developed an abiding friendship. Other brothers from a wide array of ethnicities soon joined. The McDonald's meetings, in the context of true brotherhood, led to important conversations and heartfelt sharing.

---

1. I'm thankful to Isaac Adams for these insights in an email message on December 4, 2019.

The two men started to lovingly verbalize their feeling of exile.

It launched a movement of diversity in our church.

Lament in the Minority Community

In part 3 I'm going to address the role of lament in racial reconciliation for minority brothers and sisters. After walking through the basics of lament and applying it to majority culture, I want to speak to fellow Christians who do not share my skin color.

However, let me be honest: I'm a bit nervous.

My heart is ahead of my experience and knowledge. I've spent a lot of time listening to minority church members, hearing their stories, and reading widely. But a large gap still exists in my understanding.

I'm not writing as an expert.

Yet I feel a responsibility to be a good pastor—to help people apply biblical principles in their lives beyond the reach of my firsthand experience. My minority brothers and sisters have encouraged me to do this even more. I'll try. But I think it's important to acknowledge where I'm coming from as we move into part 3 of this book.

I also need to be clear that I'm not calling minority Christians to merely lament. I believe lament prayers are vital, but they aren't all-sufficient. Building relationships, honest conversations, and working to bring change are equally important.

I've been saying that the vision for this book is that lament opens a door for racial reconciliation. It's a place to start—for both majority and minority Christians. We all need to love, listen, lament, learn, and leverage for the sake of the ethnic unity of the gospel.

In this chapter, we'll see how lament is the language of exiles, a way to honestly express pain and lovingly protest the brokenness in the world. This is especially important for minority believers to understand and apply.

Let's start by considering what it means to be an exile.

Biblical Exiles

Throughout the Old and New Testaments God's people find themselves in exile. In the Old Testament the exile is physical. In the New Testament it is spiritual. They are similar but not identical.

An exile is an outsider. In the Old Testament, "exile refers to the state of being away from one's native land."[2] Exiles are displaced from their home, or they experience isolation from a place where they should be welcomed. The people of God often faced the reality of living in a foreign land. Particular names come to mind: Joseph in Egypt, David in the wilderness, and Daniel in Babylon. These are great examples of faithfulness to God in the crucible of physical, cultural, or spiritual displacement. At other times, the entire nation experienced exile. The mass deportation of Jews connected to the Assyrian invasion of Israel and the Babylonian captivity of Judah would be prime examples.

The meaning of exile changes in the New Testament. Building upon the physical-exile model of the Old Testament, Christians are called to embrace their spiritual exile. Their "otherness" expresses itself in the contrast between their Christlike conduct in an often hostile world. The apostle Paul reminds the church at Philippi that their citizenship is in heaven (Phil. 3:20). The writer of Hebrews encourages seeking the city yet to come (Heb. 13:14). Peter addresses believers as "sojourners and exiles" while giving specific instructions for cultural engagement (1 Pet. 2:9–17). Spiritual exile represents the norm for new covenant believers.

The gospel redeems our "outsider" status.

Exiled as Minorities

If you're a minority Christian, I would guess you intuitively know what it feels like to be an exile. It's a tragic part of our nation's history for African Americans in particular. If you are black and trace your lineage,

---

2. Benjamin M. Austin and Jonathan Sutter, "Exile," in *Lexham Theological Wordbook*, ed. Douglas Mangum, Derek R. Brown, and Rachel Klippenstein (Bellingham, WA: Lexham, 2014).

you'll likely find that your ancestors didn't come to the United States willingly. They were probably part of the twelve-to-fifteen million people forcibly trafficked over the Atlantic from the 1600s to the 1800s.

What's more, if you are an African American who lives in a northern city like Chicago, Detroit, Indianapolis, or Pittsburgh, there's a good chance your parents or grandparents fled the South between 1915 and 1970. Over the course of sixty years, six million black southerners moved north fleeing segregation and the domestic terrorism of lynching. It's called the Great Migration. It dwarfs the 1850 gold rush (one hundred thousand) and the 1930 dust bowl migration (three hundred thousand).[3] Isabel Wilkerson, in her book *The Warmth of Other Suns*, says: "They would cross into alien lands with fast, new ways of speaking and carrying oneself and with hard-to-figure rules and laws. . . . They did not cross the turnstiles of customs at Ellis Island. They were already citizens. But where they came from, they were not treated as such."[4]

An already exiled people experienced even more "otherness."

I wish this story were limited to American history outside the people of God. Tragically, "otherness" marks the experience of black Christians in white churches. For example, the first African American denomination was birthed in response to being "exiled." Richard Allen and Absalom Jones were pulled from their knees because they were praying in a whites-only section of a church sanctuary. After being forcibly removed from a church in "the city of brotherly love" in 1787, they established the African Methodist Episcopal Church. Unfortunately, that was just the beginning. Bryan Loritts, in *Insider Outsider*, writes: "The black church was birthed out of rejection. Just about every historic black denomination is the offspring of white folks wanting nothing to do with us."[5]

---

3. Isabel Wilkerson, *The Warmth of Other Suns: The Epic Story of America's Great Migration* (New York: Vintage, 2010), 10.

4. Wilkerson, *The Warmth of Other Suns*, 9.

5. Bryan Loritts, *Insider Outsider: My Journey as a Stranger in White Evangelicalism and My Hope for Us All* (Grand Rapids, MI: Zondervan, 2018), 64.

The African American church deeply understands the meaning of exile.

If you are a minority, I'm sure you are familiar with "exile experiences." If you live, work, worship, or attend a school where you are a statistical outsider, you are probably reminded—passively and actively—that you are not part of the majority.

As my relationships with minority brothers and sisters have deepened, I've been grieved at how often they feel this exile. And I've marveled at the grace that my minority brothers and sisters regularly display in uncomfortable or painful situations. For example, when my wife and I attended a wedding, we sat next to some African American friends at the reception. We talked about a range of subjects: vacation plans, challenges of parenting, work life, and so on. At some point in the conversation we discussed diversity. That's when my friend pointed out that they were the only nonwhite couple at the entire reception. He wasn't complaining. "It's just hard," he said.

Living in exile is not easy.

However, I've been helped when minority believers have allowed me to understand their sense of "otherness." And I've marveled at their spiritual maturity as I've listened to them lament.

While I want to do everything in my power to change the outsider status of my minority brothers and sisters, I also want to call them—perhaps you—to keep lamenting. I think there's an opportunity for prophetic witness and cultural change as God uses painful experiences to awaken the hearts of others. Even though progress is slow and perhaps resisted, I'm hopeful that minority Christians might continue to lean into reconciliation and model for majority Christians how to respond biblically to the pain of exile while working to bring change.

Please understand, I'm not suggesting minority Christians have categorically failed in this arena. A survey of African American church history would demonstrate a greater willingness to pursue reconciliation than other churches. On a more personal level, I know many minorities who have tried but who are weary and wounded. Some of my minority friends have needed to wisely pace themselves through the exhaustion implicit in this conversation. Others have taken a break from particular "spaces," waiting to engage in the future or allowing someone else to take the mantle. The next chapter will explore how to redeem that pain through the practice of lament.

"Otherness" is a poisonous fruit of sin in the world. While it should not be passively accepted, it can become a platform for gospel-centered progress.

And a potential starting point is learning to lament.

Lamenting the Pain of Exile

Lament is the language of exiles. When God's people of old experienced the pain of displacement or isolation, they poured out their souls in prayer. Lament served both as the vocalization of sorrow and as the renewal of confidence in God's care. In this way, pain is transformed into an opportunity for spiritual victory.

Lament provides a path to rise above the discouragement.

When we read exile-oriented laments in the Bible, especially the Psalms, they validate the exile experience and provide a model for how to respond. For example, Psalm 56 expresses David's fear and frustration while fleeing from Saul (1 Sam. 21:10–15). David identifies the painful injustice of his exiled life:

> Be gracious to me, O God, for man tramples on me;
>> all day long an attacker oppresses me;
> my enemies trample on me all day long,
>> for many attack me proudly. (Ps. 56:1–2)

He wrestles with injustice:

> All day long they injure my cause;
>> all their thoughts are against me for evil.

They stir up strife, they lurk;
> they watch my steps,
> as they have waited for my life.
For their crime will they escape?
> In wrath cast down the peoples, O God! (Ps. 56:5–7)

But David doesn't stop there. While laments express pain, they empathetically affirm a path to hope.

You have kept count of my tossings;
> put my tears in your bottle.
> Are they not in your book?
Then my enemies will turn back
> in the day when I call.
> This I know, that God is for me.
In God, whose word I praise,
> in the LORD, whose word I praise,
in God I trust; I shall not be afraid.
> What can man do to me? (Ps. 56:8–11)

Laments are instructive for the one praying and for those listening. James Washington, in his book *Conversations with God: Two Centuries of Prayers by African Americans*, makes this insightful statement in the introduction to his collection of prayers:

> One need only look at the prayers in this book to see that African Americans have believed that prayer is a necessity in time of crisis. Those who have been the victim of . . . "natal alienation" understand this. Prayer in the midst of the abortion of one's human, political, and social rights is an act of justice education insofar as it reminds the one who prays, and the one who overhears it, that the one praying is a child of God.[6]

---

6. James Melvin Washington, *Conversations with God: Two Centuries of Prayers by African Americans* (New York: HarperCollins, 1994), xxiv.

When the pain of exile is expressed, biblical truths and spiritual maturity are modeled. Through lament, minority Christians and churches can teach people how to live in exile. "In the midst of marginalization, [African Americans] have learned how to dwell with sadness and transform it into strength."[7]

If you are a minority, I can imagine the temptation to feel frustrated with what you've just read. Weariness and scars of the past might make you reluctant to persevere. Please, hear me out. I've seen the fruit of this firsthand. In a forum on racial reconciliation at our church, one of our elders, an African American brother who was part of the McDonald's meetings, tearfully lamented his experience at our church. His gutsy, vulnerable honesty caused us not only to understand his pain but also to marvel at his perseverance. What's more, his words brought the reality of racial division home to us. He personalized the pain of racial insensitivity. Vocalizing his sorrow created a sanctification moment and the conviction for change in our church.

When minority Christians take the risk to lament about their sense of exile, that has the potential to bring healing to their hearts and learning to their hearers. But lament helps in other ways as well.

Lament as Protest

Lament shines a light on the brokenness of the world and calls upon God to bring change. It's a form of protest. The biblical language of sorrow gives voice to the gap between the sin-cursed world in which we live and our longing for the justice of Christ's return. It expresses spiritual outrage against the effects of the fall.

Laments appropriately declare, "This isn't right."

Two examples from the Psalms powerfully demonstrate this protest. When David barely escaped a threat on his life in 1 Samuel 19, he lamented with these words:

---

7. Jemar Tisby, *The Color of Compromise: The Truth about the American Church's Complicity in Racism* (Grand Rapids, MI: Zondervan, 2019), 202.

Deliver me from my enemies, O my God;
protect me from those who rise up against me;
deliver me from those who work evil,
and save me from bloodthirsty men.

For behold, they lie in wait for my life;
fierce men stir up strife against me.
For no transgression or sin of mine, O LORD,
for no fault of mine, they run and make ready.
Awake, come to meet me, and see! (Ps. 59:1–4)

When David fled into the wilderness (1 Sam. 22 or 24), he lamented the treachery of wicked words and plans:

My soul is in the midst of lions;
I lie down amid fiery beasts—
the children of man, whose teeth are spears and arrows,
whose tongues are sharp swords. . . .

They set a net for my steps;
my soul was bowed down.
They dug a pit in my way,
but they have fallen into it themselves. (Ps. 57:4–6)

These pointed words are a form of biblical complaint that bluntly brings what is wrong into the light. This is part of the purpose and power of lament. Soong-Chan Rah, in his book *Prophetic Lament: A Call for Justice in Troubled Times*, provides this helpful summary: "Lament is an act of protest as the lamenter is allowed to express indignation and even outrage about the experience of suffering. The lamenter talks back to God and ultimately petitions him for help, in the midst of pain."[8] In chapter 2 we learned about the spirituals. This musical genre was birthed out of suffering and protest. These songs expressed

---

8. Soong-Chan Rah, *Prophetic Lament: A Call for Justice in Troubled Times* (Downers Grove, IL: InterVarsity Press, 2015), 44.

pain and outrage. Jemar Tisby explains, "The Negro spiritual put black lamentations into songs that soared upward as prayers to God to save them and grant them perseverance to exist and resist."[9]

Laments provide an instructive window into the soul. A prayer by Richard Allen, the founder of the African Methodist Episcopal Church, helps us see this:

> O, my God! In all my dangers, temporal and spiritual, I will hope in thee who are Almighty power, therefore able to relieve me; who are infinite goodness, and therefore ready and willing to assist me. . . . What, though I mourn and am afflicted here, and sigh under the miseries of this world for a time, I am sure that my tears shall one day be turned into joy, and that joy none shall take from me.[10]

Beyond prayers that are offered, lament can highlight issues over which we should be grieved. For example, Eric Mason in his book *Woke Church*, lists ten realities we need to lament. Among the issues identified are the history behind the creation of the black church, tokenism, racial insensitivity in the academy, dismissal of the black church, evangelical perception of black preachers, and the neglect of teaching on justice.[11]

Exile experiences need to be brought into the light, and the biblical language of sorrow facilitates healing and transformation. Laments protest because of what we know to be true about God as we hope for what he, through those prayers, will do in the hearts of those who listen.

Lament as Prophetic Witness

A plea to remember and reflect is central to lament. The vocalization of pain appeals to the conscience. It awakens the soul of the person

9. Tisby, *The Color of Compromise*, 202.

10. Richard Allen, "A Prayer for Hope," in *Conversations with God: Two Centuries of Prayers by African Americans*, ed. James Melvin Washington (New York: HarperCollins, 1994), 10.

11. Eric Mason, *Woke Church: An Urgent Call for Christians in America to Confront Racism and Injustice* (Chicago: Moody Publishers, 2018), 106.

lulled into the toleration of injustice or calloused toward those living in "exile." Lament helps us hear the pain of others so that we can change. It's a means of prophetic witness—declaring God's truth to his people and the world.

One of the most shocking lament psalms in the Bible was sung in Babylon. Psalm 137 laments a request from Babylonian captors to "sing us one of the songs of Zion" (v. 3). But the psalmist replies,

> How shall we sing the LORD's song
>   in a foreign land? (v. 4)

His heart is broken over the grief of his exile.

> If I forget you, O Jerusalem,
>   let my right hand forget its skill!
> Let my tongue stick to the roof of my mouth,
>   if I do not remember you,
> if I do not set Jerusalem
>   above my highest joy! (vv. 5–6)

The pain of exile causes him to weep:

> By the waters of Babylon,
>   there we sat down and wept. (v. 1)

However, this psalm is powerful not just because of its sorrow but also because of its bold request for divine justice. Theologians often call this kind of psalm "imprecatory." Psalms such as this identify injustice and call upon God to act in accordance with his word. Psalm 137 laments the complicity of the Edomites, who likely cheered at the destruction of Jerusalem. And the psalm longs for the day when God will move upon the nation of Babylon, making all wrongs right (v. 8).[12]

---

12. Readers of Ps. 137 might be understandably horrified at verse 9: "Blessed is he who takes your little ones / and dashes them against the rock." These words reflect the horrors of the Babylonian invasion. They should be read not as a statement of personal retribution but as a fulfillment of the judgment oracle from Isa. 13:16 in which Babylon meets divine justice.

Sometimes painful and shocking words are needed as a prophetic witness to awaken the conscience.

In the "Letter from Birmingham Jail," Martin Luther King Jr. strung together painful example after painful example of the African American experience:

> But when you have seen vicious mobs lynch your mothers and fathers at will and drown your sisters and brothers at whim; when you have seen hate-filled policemen curse, kick, brutalize, and even kill your black brothers and sisters with impunity; when you see the vast majority of your twenty million Negro brothers smothering in an airtight cage of poverty in the midst of an affluent society; when you suddenly find your tongue twisted and your speech stammering as you seek to explain to your six-year-old daughter why she cannot go to the public amusement park that has just been advertised on television, and see tears welling up in her little eyes when she is told that Funtown is closed to colored children, and see the depressing clouds of inferiority begin to form in her little mental sky, and see her begin to distort her little personality by unconsciously developing a bitterness toward white people; when you have to concoct an answer for a five-year-old son asking in agonizing pathos, "Daddy, why do white people treat colored people so mean?"; when you take a cross-country drive and find it necessary to sleep night after night in the uncomfortable corners of your automobile because no motel will accept you; when you are humiliated day in and day out by nagging signs reading "white" and "colored"; when your first name becomes "nigger" and your middle name becomes "boy" (however old you are) and your last name becomes "John," and when your wife and mother are never given the respected title "Mrs."; when you are harried by day and haunted by night by the fact that you are a Negro, living constantly at tiptoe stance, never knowing what to expect next, and plagued with inner fears and outer resentments; when you are

forever fighting a degenerating sense of "nobodyness"—then you will understand why we find it difficult to wait.[13]

King's letter was a prophetic witness to the personal injustice he'd observed and felt.

A contemporary example of the blending of perseverance and protest is the song by Christian hip-hop artist Trip Lee titled "Coulda Been Me." The inspiration for the song was the flood of painful emotions evoked by the officer-involved shooting of Michael Brown in Ferguson. Few moments in contemporary American history are more vivid examples of the confusing and tense environment of race relations. In the midst of protests, investigations, and cultural pundits, many majority Christians didn't fully understand the grief and trauma experienced by the minority community in Ferguson and beyond. Many white Christians failed to grasp the reason for the protests or why the shooting and aftermath affected our minority friends so deeply. I was among them.

Trip Lee risked stepping into the complicated and emotional context of Ferguson with his song. He skillfully and prophetically vocalized his pain and personal experience while reserving final judgment as information continued to emerge. The song dropped months before the Department of Justice's two reports on the shooting and the systemic problems in the city of Ferguson.

Lee did not offer a definitive verdict, but he did share a deeply personal vantage point. The song acknowledges the uncertainty of the circumstances ("Who's innocent I don't know . . . can't solve cases, won't say that I can") and even gives a shout-out to good cops. But "Coulda Been Me" also invites the listener to empathize with the pain of Lee's experience with law enforcement and the historical hurt that many minorities felt as they watched the events in Ferguson unfold.

---

13. Martin Luther King, Jr., "Letter from a Birmingham Jail—April 16, 1963," Martin Luther King, Jr. Research and Education Institute, Stanford University, accessed August 18, 2019, http://okra.stanford.edu/transcription/document_images/undecided/630416-019.pdf.

Lee pleads with us to lament with him and to resist the tendency to dismiss the resurfacing pain of African Americans as irrelevant.[14]

I remember listening to this modern-day spiritual with tears in my eyes as I heard the pain of my minority brothers and sisters at a deeper level.

Lament prophetically witnesses against the brokenness of the world. It tearfully pleads for a change of heart leading to tangible steps of progress. Lament humbly expresses the pain of exile, lovingly protests injustice—in whatever form it appears—and prophetically calls people to love, listen, lament, learn, and leverage.

If you are a minority Christian, I want to plead with you to help your majority brothers and sisters understand your sense of "exile." I can only imagine how hard it is to persevere and how tempting it might be to give up. But there's an opportunity for God to use the heartfelt communication of your exile to create change in the church. What's more, I think you might be surprised at how instructive it is for majority Christians as they witness your Christlike response.

Vocalizing your exile can be a path for change.

I've seen it happen.

While our church still has a long way to go, the McDonald's conversations led to elder discussions about racial reconciliation and leadership diversity. We hosted a Sunday evening forum for our minority church members to share about their church experience. The Civil Rights Vision Trip followed, along with a weekend theology conference and a three-week sermon series on racial reconciliation. The exile experience of these brothers led to a monthly meeting called 3DG—Diversity Discipleship Discussion Group.

Each of the African American brothers had a unique spiritual reason for coming to our church. But I know God sent them. None of them came with an agenda. But the Lord certainly had a plan that I

---

14. Trip Lee, "Coulda Been Me," Brag (website), accessed January 20, 2020, https://builtto brag.com/coulda-lyrics/.

now see more clearly. As the pastor of our church, I owe a great debt to these dearly loved brothers. They've taught me a lot. We've cried, argued, laughed, sought forgiveness, and marveled at what God is doing. It hasn't been easy, but we see God at work. Together we are attempting to help our church look and act more like the vision in Revelation 7.

I still don't know how to shepherd all the contours of their experience, but I'm trying. And here's what I know: God used their exile to accelerate racial reconciliation in our church.

LAMENT PRAYER
(Based on Ps. 137)

By the streets of Ferguson we sat and wept, when we remembered Zion. We know we are your children, Lord. We know you created black and brown lives in your image, and that those lives matter to you. And yet, they have been treated as expendable. We are afraid, Lord. Afraid to walk our own neighborhoods, afraid to drive our own vehicles, afraid that our black sons will be the next Tamir Rice or Mike Brown. We are afraid of any encounter with the very officers sworn to protect and serve us. Lord, we hear of more unarmed black people killed under suspicious circumstances every week. Though the media has moved on from these stories, we are still afraid, Lord, because no amount of respectability will protect us from those who fear our very skin.

To make matters worse, our own church members, Christian brothers and sisters, have denied our suffering. They have despised our tears and dismissed our fears as illegitimate, even unchristian. Rather than weep with us, they required that we sing songs of mirth. "Sing us one of the songs of Zion." Sing of joy, sing of happiness. But how can we sing of happiness at a time like this? If I forget your slain image bearers, if I forget your standard of justice, if I forget your love for suffering people, may my right hand forget its skill, and may I never sing again.

Lord, remember the devastation that hatred and injustice has wrought against us. Lord, remember and destroy the works of the devil. Destroy the instruments of injustice. Defeat the principality that has exploited black life in this land for so long!

In Jesus's name and for his sake. Amen.

Mika Edmondson,
pastor of New City Fellowship Church,
Grand Rapids, Michigan

Discussion Questions

1. In your own words, how would you define an exile?

2. What are some of the ways that minorities experience exile? Do you have any personal examples or experiences to share?

3. What is the connection between exile and lament?

4. How does lament function as protest?

5. As you read the "Letter from Birmingham Jail," what lessons did you learn?

6. Why is it potentially transformative for minority Christians to see their experience through the lens of exile and vocalize it through lament?

7. Where might it be helpful for these "exile laments" to be heard?

8. Consider writing out your own exile lament and sharing it with others.

8

TRIUMPH

Redeeming the Pain

If the LORD had not been my help,
  my soul would soon have lived in the land of silence.
When I thought, "My foot slips,"
  your steadfast love, O LORD, held me up.

PSALM 94:17–18

Now that we've wrestled with the cultural category of "outsider," I want to consider a more personal issue. This chapter explores how lament helps Christians redeem their hurt. I've placed this chapter in part 3 because I want to especially apply this concept to the experience of minority believers.

Don't get me wrong. What you are about to read should be applied to anyone attempting to respond biblically to the hurts pummeling his or her soul. So, if you are not a minority Christian, keep reading. There will be hurts and pain in your life to apply what follows. However, facing discrimination or enduring a racially loaded comment will probably not be the most significant challenge you face. But there will be others. This chapter can help you know what to do with that pain.

But it also can help you further empathize with your minority brothers and sisters. It should cause you to pray more fervently and to walk alongside them.

Layers of Pain

Still, my primary audience for this chapter is minority Christian readers. And I don't have to convince you about the deep layers of hurt connected to racial issues.

As I've developed deeper relationships with minority Christians, I've learned that the personal pain of racism, prejudice, and injustice runs deep. My friends and church members hide it well. They have to; it's a survival strategy. But every once in a while, I've earned enough relational capital that I'm allowed to hear a deeper level of pain. One minority church member tearfully told me, "You are the first white man I've been able to really trust." I hope that continues and builds through this chapter.

Disclaimers

Before I go any further, let me give you a few disclaimers.

First, I'm not writing out of personal experience with racially oriented hurt. I can't think of a time I've been racially slurred. I've never felt the looming clouds of "otherness" or the judgmental looks of condescension because of the color of my skin.

The second disclaimer is more of an affirmation. I believe the hurt from racism, prejudice, and injustice is very real—more so than what most white Christians realize. I was struck by the weight of Eric Mason's words: "Most African-Americans have had at least two life-altering experiences that are burned into their memory—the moment they realized they were black and the moment they realized that was a problem."[1] I'm sure this experience applies to all of our black brothers and sisters at some level. And I'm confident that you've encountered people who have refused to acknowledge the reality of your pain. Please know, from the outset, that's not where I'm coming from.

Further, we'll explore how lament can be useful for redeeming racial hurt. As I've examined the African American church tradition, I've found lament to be a familiar language. I referenced this in chapter 2 with regard to spirituals. By suggesting new ways to apply this biblical language of sorrow in this chapter, I'm not blazing some new trail for minority brothers and sisters. More likely, our examination may offer categories to understand your experience and sorrow. You'll probably find yourself saying, "Ahhh, *that's* what I've been doing." Lament may not be new. But I hope you'll go even deeper.

Finally, while this chapter will address how to lament the hurts and injustice, I want to assure you that I'm not suggesting a posture of resigned acceptance. Throughout history, the Bible has been used to convince minorities to merely accept their lot in life. Whether through an overapplication of the doctrine of God's sovereignty or the use of texts like Colossians 3:22 or Ephesians 6:5–6, church history is littered with examples of spiritualized justifications for the status quo. My goal is not to repeat the same mistake. Rather, I want to show you how lament validates your struggle, provides a path for healing, and positions you to bring change. I hope to show you how lamenting your hurts empowers you to persevere through the long and emotionally painful journey of racial reconciliation.

How does a minority Christian stay engaged in this exhausting conversation? Where should you go with your hurts when your soul is tired and weary? How do you talk to God about injustice so that you can model a Christlike prophetic balance of grace and truth? Here's one way forward.

---

1. Eric Mason, *Woke Church: An Urgent Call for Christians in America to Confront Racism and Injustice* (Chicago: Moody Publishers, 2018), 27.

How to Lament

I introduced the idea of biblical lament in the first chapter. We started by defining lament as a prayer in pain that leads to trust. And I gave four steps:

- Turn—choosing to talk to God about our pain
- Complain—candidly praying about the struggles, questions, and disappointments
- Ask—boldly calling upon God to be true to his promises
- Trust—reaffirming what we believe about God

This four-step process is not only a method to examine lament psalms but also a way for prayers to be offered when "the cares of my heart are many" (Ps. 94:19). Remember the laments on the Civil Rights Vision Trip? If you're a minority Christian, I hope you'll learn to embrace this minor-key song and use it to express your hurt.

As you practice lament, you'll find that it validates your struggle and pushes you to renew your trust in God. And my ultimate hope (the aim of this book) is for you to stay engaged in the racial-reconciliation conversation. Instead of "faking it" or being overcome with frustration, I hope to help you run the race set before you as you look to Jesus (Heb. 12:1–2).

Psalm 94: "Rise Up, O Judge of the Earth!"

There are at least fifty lament psalms in the Bible. They empathize and empower us to vocalize our struggle so that godly perseverance will mark our lives.

Let's use the fourfold lens to examine Psalm 94. I hope this becomes a model for looking at other laments and the way you can pray when you are responding to the pains of racism, prejudice, or injustice.

Turn to Prayer

Psalm 94 mourns the brutality of the wicked (v. 3) toward the weak and oppressed. The proud evildoers have no concern for the fear of

God (vv. 6–7). At the same time, "the song asks God to take action to protect the faithful. . . . It strengthens the pious to endure this oppression without losing heart or going over to join the wicked."[2]

Laments show us how hurting and mistreated people talk to God.

The first two verses are classic examples of turning to God in prayer when injustice rears its ugly head. The psalmist appeals to the "God of vengeance," the "judge of the earth" to "repay to the proud what they deserve" (vv. 1–2). If you read verse 1 carefully, the word "vengeance" likely jumps off the page. We don't normally pray that way. Let me explain what's happening here.

When we experience injustice, we rightly desire for it to be corrected. Some Christians think forgiveness negates the need for justice. However, this is a misunderstanding of both the gospel and what forgiveness entails. God forgives us because Jesus satisfied the demands of divine justice (see Rom. 3:21–26; 2 Cor. 5:21). One day Jesus is going to return as the great Judge. That's why the martyrs lament the delay of justice in Revelation 6:10: "How long before you will judge and avenge our blood on those who dwell on the earth?" Christians long for the day when the King of kings, called "Faithful and True," brings complete justice to earth (Rev. 19:11). That desire is right.

However, Christians are commanded never to take their own revenge.

> Beloved, never avenge yourselves, but leave it to the wrath of God, for it is written, "Vengeance is mine, I will repay, says the Lord." To the contrary, "if your enemy is hungry, feed him; if he is thirsty, give him something to drink; for by so doing you will heap burning coals on his head." Do not be overcome by evil, but overcome evil with good. (Rom. 12:19–21)

Vengeance belongs to God. Additionally, God has appointed earthly authorities for the distribution of justice.

---

2. *ESV Study Bible*, ed. Wayne Grudem, J. I. Packer, C. John Collins, and Thomas R. Schreiner (Wheaton, IL: Crossway, 2008), 1057.

Let every person be subject to the governing authorities. For there is no authority except from God, and those that exist have been instituted by God. Therefore whoever resists the authorities resists what God has appointed, and those who resist will incur judgment. . . . For he is God's servant for your good. But if you do wrong, be afraid, for he does not bear the sword in vain. For he is the servant of God, an avenger who carries out God's wrath on the wrongdoer. (Rom. 13:1–2, 4)

Why does this matter as it relates to racial reconciliation? Three reasons. First, this lament psalm validates the concern with injustice. Whether it's historical or personal, this psalm identifies that talking to God about unfairness and mistreatment was part of the inspired word of God. Second, Psalm 94 shows us an appeal made not only because of personal wrongs but also because the divinely given system of justice was not working. The fall affected God-ordained authorities and systems. That's doubly scary. Third, reading this psalm helps us see what to do with our frustrations and deep concern. This is where I think lament can be uniquely helpful.

Turning to God in prayer and talking to him about injustice positions us to put away personal revenge. It frees Christians to model Christlikeness as they seek to bring change.

Lament is a prayer in pain that leads to trust so that you can persevere in racial reconciliation.

Offer Your Complaints

The second element we see in Psalm 94 is the candid expression of pain through complaint. This may not be familiar territory. It's important to know that biblical complaint—telling God what is wrong—is central to lament. And it can be extremely helpful to your soul.

In Psalm 94 we read the following complaints:

- "How long shall the wicked exult?" (v. 3).
- "They pour out their arrogant words" (v. 4).

- "They kill the widow and the sojourner, / and murder the fatherless" (v. 6).
- "They say, 'The LORD does not see; / the God of Jacob does not perceive'" (v. 7).

Complaint talks bluntly to God about your pain.

This text is useful for those moments in your life when you feel like you are being mistreated. You can use this text to channel your frustration and talk to God about it. Hip-hop artist and preacher Trip Lee models lament in his song "I Don't Know" ("IDK"). He uses Psalm 13, a lament, to process his grief over the death of a friend's son and a series of racially loaded shootings. Reflecting on the transformative power of lament, he says, "I want people to contemplate what it looks like to bring our complaints before God—what it looks like to doubt him, but to strive to wrestle with him and see what it looks like to trust him during those hard times."[3]

Psalm 94 is also helpful in the struggle with systemic injustice—when sinful depravity is written into laws or accepted as culturally normal. Psalm 94:20 says this:

Can wicked rulers be allied with you,
    those who frame injustice by statute?

One of the challenges in the racial-reconciliation conversation is this issue. You don't have to look far into American or church history to find examples of injustice that became systematized or ingrained in our culture. The civil rights movement fought hard against the racism that dominated American society. Psalm 94 acknowledges that our depravity is more than an individual concern. Injustice can be framed by statute.

Sin slithers its way into the halls of power, legislation, and our culture.

When I've quoted this verse to my minority friends, I often encounter surprised relief that the Bible talks this way. I know there is an extensive and intense debate about systemic racism in the past and present.

---

3. Rebecca Van Noord, "A Conversation with Hip Hop Artist and Preacher Trip Lee," *Bible Study Magazine*—July/August 2017, http://www.biblestudymagazine.com/julyaugust-2017-trip-lee.

However, for too long minorities have endured opposition or suspicion when talking about this frustration. It's important to recognize that this lament acknowledges systemic injustice as something the Bible mourns.

Lament is powerful because it talks to God about what we feel. Biblical complaint provides a spiritual process for working through the layers of pain. It validates the frustration. Jemar Tisby comments, "Racism has inflicted incalculable suffering on black people throughout the history of the United States, and in such a context lament is not only understandable but necessary."[4]

Lament expresses outrage.

As lament becomes a more familiar step in your response to hurt, it can help to prevent the poisonous mist of bitterness from infecting your life. Lament validates a painful experience without making it your identity. Michael Card says: "We all carry deep within ourselves a pressurized reservoir of tears. It takes only the right key at the right time to unlock them . . . In God's perfect time, through lament, when these tears are released, they can form a vast healing flood."[5] That's true for any hurt, but especially the hurt of racism or prejudice.

Minority brothers and sisters, while I don't know firsthand the sting of prejudicial words or the sense that the system is working against me, I hope you'll embrace the power of biblical complaint. The Psalms are full of honest words through which we talk to God about our hurt. Rather than denying or despairing amid the pain, you can discover the healing grace of talking to God about the depth of your sorrow so that you can be strengthened to continue to respond in Christlikeness and help the church.

Ask Boldly

Laying out our complaints is only the halfway point through the lament process. Psalm 94 shows us the value of calling upon God to

---

4. Jemar Tisby, *The Color of Compromise: The Truth about the American Church's Complicity in Racism* (Grand Rapids, MI: Zondervan, 2019), 179.

5. Michael Card, *A Sacred Sorrow: Reaching Out to God in the Lost Language of Lament* (Colorado Springs: NavPress, 2005), 86.

act. Asking boldly moves from "what is wrong?" to "what is true?" It reminds our hearts about the promises of the Bible. In this way, lament cuts through the disorienting cloud of hurt and the feelings of powerlessness.

Lament drops an emotional anchor in the character of God.

Psalm 94 makes a number of promise-affirming statements. In verses 9–11, the psalmist affirms God's power:

> He who planted the ear, does he not hear?
> He who formed the eye, does he not see?
> He who disciplines the nations, does he not rebuke?
> He who teaches man knowledge—
>> the LORD—knows the thoughts of man,
>> that they are but a breath.

When life feels out of control, it's good to celebrate God's authority.

The psalmist doesn't stop there. He continues to remind his heart and those who sing this lament that God is at work, even in the midst of injustice. Psalm 94 embraces the spiritual value of hardship (v. 12) while affirming God's ability to give his people rest (v. 13). The writer celebrates the Lord's promise to not forsake his people (v. 14) and longs for the day when "justice will return to the righteous" (v. 15). He declares his belief in God as his defender (v. 16). The psalmist takes refuge in the safety of God's promises:

> If the LORD had not been my help,
>> my soul would soon have lived in the land of silence.
> When I thought, "My foot slips,"
>> your steadfast love, O LORD, held me up.
> When the cares of my heart are many,
>> your consolations cheer my soul. (vv. 17–19)

In this way, lament helps with perspective. This is part of the reason why Sunday services in the African American church have been so important and lively—a tradition that remains to this day. Sunday is a refuge from the unfairness of the culture. Perhaps you grew up in a traditional church where services were long, dressing up was the norm, and titles ("Deacon Jones") were important. Sunday in the African American church meant dignity, worth, and value—a time to reconnect with the truths underneath the hard experiences.

In a speech titled "Where Do We Go from Here?" Martin Luther King Jr. echoed the hope-filled connection to eternal realities beyond the struggle for civil rights:

> When our days become dreary with low-hovering clouds of despair, and when our nights become darker than a thousand midnights, let us remember that there is a creative force in this universe working to pull down the gigantic mountains of evil, a power that is able to make a way out of no way and transform dark yesterdays into bright tomorrows. Let us realize that the arc of the moral universe is long, but it bends toward justice.[6]

Let me encourage you to use lament to provide direction for your soul. Based upon the promises of Scripture, ask God to help you.

Remind your heart what is true.

Choose to Trust

Now we come to the final step in lament—trust. This is where all laments are designed to lead. They move us from the trauma of pain to a renewed confidence in God. But this is more than an emotional catharsis. Lament provides a path for hurt so we can live faithfully. It creates a way to persevere under the prevailing clouds of hardship.

---

6. Martin Luther King, Jr., "Where Do We Go from Here? Address Delivered at the Eleventh Annual SCLC Convention, August 16, 1967," Martin Luther King, Jr. Research and Education Institute, Stanford University, accessed September 13, 2019, https://kinginstitute.stanford.edu/king-papers/documents/where-do-we-go-here-address-delivered-eleventh-annual-sclc-convention.

Every lament features a turning point.[7] Usually it's connected to words like *but, even so,* or *then.* It's where the psalmist reaffirms confidence in God so that he can pursue righteousness the right way. Here is what hopeful trust in both God's power and his ability to bring justice looks like in Psalm 94:

> But the LORD has become my stronghold,
> > and my God the rock of my refuge.
> He will bring back on them their iniquity
> > and wipe them out for their wickedness;
> > the LORD our God will wipe them out. (vv. 22–23)

The right posture allows you to speak prophetically from a position of confident hope in God. Dhati Lewis, in his book *Advocates: The Narrow Path to Racial Reconciliation,* expresses the goal:

> I am certainly not saying to let injustice run rampant. What I want to get at here is the posture of our hearts, the motivations for our actions, and the ways we trust (or don't trust) God. . . . [We] need to trust that God is just, that he will ultimately and finally act on the side of the oppressed, and that [we] are called, even in [our] work toward justice, to submit to the commands of Jesus.[8]

This perspective is essential for the effectiveness of your engagement in racial reconciliation. It is how you follow the example of Jesus.

The ugly strongholds of prejudice and injustice are painful and discouraging. Lament isn't a quick fix. Life is still hard. But this minor-key song provides a way to address the ache of your heart so that you can continue to stay in the calling to pursue reconciliation—even when you are the one who has been hurt.

---

7. Psalm 88 may be the exception, although many scholars believe Pss. 88 and 89 are meant to be read together.

8. Dhati Lewis, *Advocates: The Narrow Path to Racial Reconciliation* (Nashville: B&H, 2019), loc. 526 of 1987, Kindle.

Practical Steps

Let me suggest a few ways you might apply what we've learned in this chapter.

Run to Jesus

It might sound trite, but to redeem our pain we have to keep running to our Redeemer. Instead of being lulled into the trap of deep-seated resentment or bitterness, we need to rehearse who Jesus is and what that means. The more I've studied lament, the more thankful I am that Jesus is acquainted with grief (Isa. 53:3). He understands the struggles of our broken humanity (Heb. 4:15). When you are grieving over another painful rejection or being despised, turn your heart toward the Son of God who empathizes. Run to him. Use your pain to drive you toward the Savior. Don't allow sorrow to win. Let grief lead you to renew your love for the man of sorrows.

Practice Lament

We have examined only one lament psalm in this chapter. There are over forty more you can explore for examples of turning, complaining, asking, and trusting. Take some time to read the other laments like the ones listed in appendix 1. Become proficient in lamenting hurts and pains so that the language is familiar when you need it for more traumatic moments. I've provided a worksheet in appendix 2 to serve as a guide. When you are deeply hurting over the pain of injustice or prejudice, make lament your first step. Embrace it as a spiritual resource.

Stay Engaged

Pain creates a desire to retreat. The psalmist said:

> Oh, that I had wings like a dove!
> I would fly away and be at rest. (Ps. 55:6)

Part of the reason I wrote this book was to help minority Christians persevere through the challenges of reconciliation. At times I've seen weariness create new barriers to ethnic and racial harmony. Minority Christians bear a heavy load in this conversation. And I'm hopeful that you'll be among those who stay engaged and whom the Lord uses to bring Christlike change.

The enemy desires the church to remain divided. He's working to create new misunderstandings and hurts. It takes courage and godliness to pursue reconciliation, especially if you are the one mistreated. And while lament doesn't fix everything, it can help.

You can redeem the pain.

And talking to God about it is a good place to start.

LAMENT PRAYER

O God, as the deer pants for deep streams of waters, so do the souls of your people long to see racial and ethnic conciliation in our churches and in society. Our souls pant for you, O God, the living God, to rid our churches of all forms of overt and covert racism, ethnocentrism, and ethnic and racial prejudice. We cry out to you, O God, to enable us, your people, to personify the prayer of unity for which Jesus, your Son, prayed, and to pursue and call sinners to the vertical and horizontal reconciliation for which he died and was resurrected.

O God, our Father, it seems as though the more we, your people, pray for these things and the more we attempt to walk in the power of the Spirit to pursue these things, the stronger racism and ethnic division grow in our churches and in our communities. And many of your people, O God, suffer in various forms from the wicked acts of their enemies outside the church and inside the church because their enemies resist the gospel's call and the efforts of your people to unify all things and all people in Christ. This suffering, O God, makes both your people and their enemies ask: Where is God in his people's suffering? Has God forgotten them? Why do his people go mourning because of oppression at the hands of their enemies if in fact the efforts of his people to apply the gospel of Jesus Christ to racism are indeed encouraged by, taught by, and empowered by God, his Christ, his Spirit, and his word?

Yet, O God, in the face of the suffering that will always come as a result of sin's power to use racism, ethnocentrism, and racial prejudice in both the church and society, we, your people, who have placed our hope in Jesus's death and resurrection, proclaim to our own souls and to the souls of the weary saints of God: Do not be cast down, you weary saints, and may your souls not be in turmoil within you. But hope in your God! For we will again praise him, because he's the God of our salvation. He is our God, who has saved us through faith in his Christ, and who will reconcile and unify all things and all people to himself and to one another in his time through Jesus Christ, our Lord.

In the name of the crucified, resurrected, and glorified Christ I pray. Amen.

Jarvis Williams,
associate professor of New Testament interpretation
at the Southern Baptist Theological Seminary,
Louisville, Kentucky

Discussion Questions

1. Can you relate to the notion of layers of pain? How do layers make pain more complicated and challenging to address?

2. Why was it important for me to make some disclaimers?

3. What are some barriers for minority Christians in praying lament prayers about race-related pain?

4. Why would it be tempting to fall into the ditch of denial or despair when it comes to this topic?

5. Make a list of heartfelt "complaints" about the pain of racism and prejudice. If appropriate, share this list with a friend, a spouse, or your Bible study.

6. Make another list of biblical promises that you need to pray. Share your list and explain why those promises are uniquely meaningful for walking through racial reconciliation.

7. What action steps do you need to take in light of this chapter? How does lament liberate you to stay engaged in this process?

9

BELIEVE

Dare to Hope Again

I will never forget this awful time. . . .
Yet I still dare to hope.

LAMENTATIONS 3:20–21 NLT

"Brother, I'm sorry that happened. It wasn't right. Would you let us pray for you?"

Somewhat reluctantly, a white church member named Aaron and a friend walked to the front of the room of a Sunday morning meeting of the Diversity Discipleship Discussion Group (3DG). Two chairs were pulled out. The diverse leadership team of 3DG hugged them. After Aaron and a friend were seated, the leaders laid their hands on them and began to pray.

Aaron's journey to that meeting began weeks earlier. He attended our church's first forum on racial reconciliation. He was deeply troubled—even angry. He fired off a long email to me. We met in my office for a tense meeting.

I learned there was more to Aaron's story.

As we talked, I discovered Aaron grew up as a white minority. In his neighborhood and high school, he was regularly singled out, mocked, and even assaulted because he was white. He felt the sting of prejudicial injustice in his most formative years. As he shared his experience, I tried to listen and empathize with his struggle. We discussed a wide range of topics. I attempted to reassure him that our church's emphasis on racial harmony was rooted in the gospel and the Great Commission. I wasn't sure Aaron was interested in understanding. He was mad. He was hurt.

I closed the meeting by issuing him a challenge: "Aaron, I want you to consider attending the Diversity Discipleship Discussion Group." I didn't think he would dare take that step. But he did.

Aaron stood in the 3DG classroom to share his experience. He fully expected to be rejected—again. When he opened up about the prejudice and unfairness directed at him, his voice cracked. The hatred, pain, and struggle of over a decade rose to the surface.

And that's when it happened.

A minority leader of 3DG empathized with him. He identified with the injustice of Aaron's experience. And that's when he said, "Would you let us pray for you?" The effect was profound. Here is Aaron in his own words:

> I cannot describe the change that one interaction brought about in my heart, or how healing it was to have my African American brothers and sisters praying over me. God used those relationships to both expose the raw pain and emotions that I had buried for decades and to replace those pains with love and contentment. Those relationships have made the conversations about "racial harmony" or "ethnic reconciliation" not only safe, but positive. I've grown to truly empathize with the pain my minority brothers and sisters feel, because they in turn have recognized and empathized

with mine. Because of what has happened through both the 3DG group and my relationships outside of it, my mind and heart have totally changed.[1]

Aaron left the room a different man. And I'm happy to tell you he's not the only one. By God's grace there are other stories of reconciliation happening in our church. We still have a long way to go, and I know that some people are not supportive—either in public or in private. But one conversation at a time, God is working.

The key was the grace-filled response by the minority leaders. They modeled Christlikeness. It created the impetus for change in a fellow church member.

I hope you'll follow their example.

In order for racial reconciliation to happen in the church, we need Christians who refuse to give up hope. Despite the historical challenges, personal hurts, and slowness of progress, we must persevere with Christlike resolve. In this chapter, I want to encourage you—especially minority believers—to keep believing in God's ability to bring change. I hope to show you how lament can help you in that journey.

Dare to Hope

Jeremiah is often called the weeping prophet. His ministry was marked by a relentless call for the nation of Judah to change its ways. However, the people refused to listen. The consequences were devastating. The clouds of hardship descended on the city of Jerusalem. The armies of Babylon destroyed the temple and humiliated the nation. The situation could not have been much worse. It called for lamentation.

The longest lament in the Bible is the book of Lamentations. It wrestles with the tension of faithful living when life is hard. Lamentations demonstrates how believers find hope when the looming clouds of painful circumstances refuse to leave. And that's why it's uniquely helpful.

---

1. Email interview, April 1, 2019, used by permission.

The apex of the book is the third chapter. The two chapters before and after recount the devastating and ongoing effects of the Babylonian invasion. But Jeremiah refuses to give in to despair. He chooses to believe and live upon God's grace. Here's what it sounds like in the New Living Translation:

> The thought of my suffering and homelessness
>   is bitter beyond words.
> I will never forget this awful time,
>   as I grieve over my loss.
> Yet I still dare to hope
>   when I remember this:
>
> The faithful love of the LORD never ends!
>   His mercies never cease.
> Great is his faithfulness;
>   his mercies begin afresh each morning.
> I say to myself, "The LORD is my inheritance;
>   therefore, I will hope in him!" (Lam. 3:19–24)

I love the phrase "dare to hope," especially when you consider the circumstances in which this lament is written.

Few things are riskier than starting to think things will change for the better. And I would imagine that some minority readers might be weary of the on-again, off-again nature of racial reconciliation. Perhaps you've seen conversations start, only to be shut down. Maybe you've felt the sting of disappointment with what your Christian friends post, comment, or like on social media. You may feel misunderstood or unable to be honest with family, coworkers, or fellow Christians. Perhaps you hoped a particular church was going to be different, only to be disappointed. You may even feel that way with this book. I hope not, but I wouldn't be surprised if that was the case at some level.

The challenge, of course, is that weariness can lead to hopelessness. While I've not wrestled with prejudice directed at me, I've felt a lack of hope as I've walked through grief or the pains of pastoral ministry. When this mindset sets in, two things happen. First, you begin to justify attitudes or actions that aren't Christlike. It's easy to become defensive or edgy. In the midst of a social-media frenzy about a racial topic, Bryan Loritts tweeted a helpful caution: "Don't just be prophetic in your denunciations of racism, also be pastoral. We need prophetic courage and pastoral conversations."[2] Hopelessness can breed an unhelpful tone or ungodly words.

Second, a lack of hope hinders true change in Christians, the church, and the culture. Hopelessness tempts us to remain silent or to tolerate injustice. Why speak up or "stick your neck out" when you think it'll make no difference? Once you've resigned yourself that nothing's going to change, it's easy to retreat. Patient endurance and bold actions are critical to progress in reconciliation. Hope is essential to both. During a visit to the National Memorial for Peace and Justice in Montgomery, I was struck by these words mounted on the wall: "Hopelessness is the enemy of justice."

As we look at the darkness of the present and consider the challenges of the future, what might we dare to hope for? What do we need to believe? How might lament help minority Christians not to grow weary in doing good (Gal. 6:9)? Let me suggest four hopes for the future.

God Will Help You

The first hopeful promise flows out of the third chapter of Lamentations. It reminds us that we can dare to hope by believing that God will always provide the spiritual resource of grace. Believers never exhaust the supply of God's ability to help them. The passage says that God's

---

2. Bryan Loritts, "Don't just be prophetic in your denunciations of racism, also be pastoral," Twitter, April 12, 2019, 12:56 p.m., https://twitter.com/bcloritts/status/1116792293187436544.

"mercies begin afresh each morning" (Lam. 3:23 NLT). I wouldn't be surprised if that's a familiar thought for you. But I think it takes on new meaning when you consider the circumstances in which Jeremiah wrote this lament. While he acknowledges the difficulty of the moment, he also affirms that God is able to supply what he needs to persevere. That was an important promise for Jeremiah to affirm, especially when the circumstances of life were discouraging.

This is uniquely important for minority Christians, due to the exhaustion and frustration often connected to racial reconciliation. In view of the history, pain, and lack of progress in some areas, it would be easy to give up. Or it would be understandable to become deeply skeptical of any progress out of a sense of self-protection. After all, few things are more hurtful than being disappointed—yet again.

Lamentations 3 reminds us that God is able to help the discouraged and the weary. His mercy and steadfast love are deeper than your disappointments. Persevering with hope in racial reconciliation when you are a minority requires a deep faith in God's ability to give you grace. Whether it is receiving the grace of God's love for you, the grace of covering offenses in love, the grace of honestly sharing your hurts, or the grace of working tirelessly to bring change, minority Christians need this heart orientation to stay hopeful.

A survey of history would demonstrate that this mindset was part of the African American historical struggle with racism and injustice. Howard Thurman, in his book *Deep River*, identifies this perspective in the spirituals:

> They express the profound conviction that God was not done with them, that God was not done with life. The consciousness that God had not exhausted his resources or better still that the vicissitudes of life could not exhaust God's resources, did not ever leave them. This is the secret to their ascendency over circumstances and the basis of their assurances concerning death and life. The aware-

ness of the presence of a God who was personal and intimate and active was the central fact of life and around it all the details of life and destiny were integrated.[3]

You can dare to hope that God never runs out of grace for whatever you face.

Hardship Can Be Transformative

On a recent trip to Washington, DC, I visited the Martin Luther King Jr. Memorial. A statue of King is cut from a massive piece of granite that appears to have broken free from a mountain in the background. Etched into the memorial are these words: "Out of a mountain of despair, a stone of hope." King embodied the belief that society could be transformed by self-sacrifice. This conviction was born out of the teaching of the Bible.

The apostle Paul lamented the sufferings he endured while helping the Corinthian church to understand the life-giving effect. Notice his honest lament and his hopeful perspective:

> For we do not want you to be unaware, brothers, of the affliction we experienced in Asia. For we were so utterly burdened beyond our strength that we despaired of life itself. (2 Cor. 1:8)

> We are afflicted in every way, but not crushed; perplexed, but not driven to despair; persecuted, but not forsaken; struck down, but not destroyed; always carrying in the body the death of Jesus, so that the life of Jesus may also be manifested in our bodies. For we who live are always being given over to death for Jesus' sake, so that the life of Jesus also may be manifested in our mortal flesh. So death is at work in us, but life in you. (2 Cor. 4:8–12)

Paul recognized that hardships can produce life in other people. Patiently enduring inspires others. Suffering can bring conviction.

---

3. Howard Thurman, *Deep River and the Negro Spiritual Speaks of Life and Death* (Richmond, IN: Friends United, 1975), 37–38.

The civil rights movement effectively leveraged suffering for the purpose of societal change. But it required willing sacrifice and deep commitment. At the National Civil Rights Museum, I found the following ten commandments of the nonviolent ethic:

I hereby pledge myself, my person, and body to the nonviolent movement. I will keep the following ten commandments:

1. Meditate daily on the teachings and life of Jesus.
2. Remember always that the nonviolent movement in Birmingham seeks justice and reconciliation, not victory.
3. Walk and talk in the manner of love, for God is love.
4. Pray daily to be used by God in order that all men might be free.
5. Sacrifice personal wishes in order that all men might be free.
6. Observe with both friend and foe the ordinary rules of courtesy.
7. Seek to perform regular service for others and for the world.
8. Refrain from violence of fist, tongue, or heart.
9. Strive to be in good spiritual and bodily health.
10. Follow the directions of the movement and the captain on a demonstration.

Suffering and the cries of lament are powerful tools in the hand of God for change. Don't forget that Jesus's lament "Why have you forsaken me?" created a pathway for reconciliation between us and God. The apostle Paul quotes a lament in Romans 8:36—"for your sake we are being killed all the day long"—before affirming the believer's victory in Christ: "No, in all these things we are more than conquerors through him who loved us" (8:37). Suffering can create life-giving change for both the individual and those who see his or her example.

Don't forget that hardship can be transformative.

God Changes Hearts

While suffering and injustice hang in the air, lament is the language that appeals to God to intervene. Lament looks to God to change people's hearts. In the Psalms, we find appeals to God for transformation through judgment. The lament of Psalm 83:16 says,

> Fill their faces with shame,
>> that they may seek your name, O LORD.

Dan Estes, in his commentary on the Psalms, helps us understand the intent of this lament: "This in effect is asking the Lord to act with grace to save those who have conspired to exterminate Israel. . . . The nations need to experience the dishonor and shame they had planned for Israel in order that with their pride broken they may turn humbly to the Lord."[4]

Those who lament put their hope in God's ability to bring change.

Lurking under the surface of racial reconciliation are hidden heart ailments. Whether you encounter the projection of superiority, a willful ignorance, or simple self-centeredness, it's easy to lose hope that true and lasting change can happen. And yet it's important to remember that no heart is beyond God's reach.

You may find yourself weary with the insensitivities of what people say. Perhaps you feel exasperated, sensing that hardened hearts can never be softened. Let me encourage you to keep talking to the Lord and appealing to him for change, especially for those who seem beyond hope. You might be surprised what God will do.

In American history, few political figures are more associated with racism than George Wallace, the forty-fifth governor of Alabama. Wallace's rise to the highest office in his state was fueled by his undying support of segregation. His 1963 inaugural address featured this thundering and infamous statement: "Segregation now. Segregation tomorrow. Segregation forever." Wallace was the face and voice of opposition to the civil rights movement. Martin Luther King Jr. called him the most dangerous racist in America.[5] However, while Wallace

---

4. Daniel J. Estes, *Psalms 73–150*, vol. 13 of *The New American Commentary* (Nashville: B&H, 2019), 126.

5. Jonathan Capeheart, "How Segregationist George Wallace Became a Model for Racial Reconciliation: 'Voices of the Movement' Episode 6," *Washington Post*, May 16, 2015, https://www

was running for his party's nomination for president in 1972, he was shot at a political rally in Maryland. The bullet lodged in his spine, leaving him paralyzed at the waist.

While an assassin's bullet prevented him from ever walking again, Wallace's injury led to a change of heart. He began a seven-year journey that eventually led to a dramatic Sunday in 1979.

Wallace arrived unannounced at Dexter Avenue Baptist Church, where Martin Luther King Jr. pastored years earlier. The church sits just a block from the Alabama State Capitol in Montgomery. After Wallace was wheeled up front, he made a stunning statement: "I have learned what suffering means. In a way that was impossible [before the shooting], I think I can understand something of the pain black people have come to endure. I know I contributed to that pain, and I can only ask your forgiveness."[6] As Wallace was wheeled out, the church began to sing "Amazing Grace."[7] This was not the only time Wallace acknowledged his wrongdoing. He spent the remaining years of his life speaking at events and meeting with civil rights leaders, seeking their forgiveness and pursuing reconciliation.

Wallace's daughter, Peggy Wallace Kennedy, believes the seeds of the governor's transformation were planted by a black congresswoman named Shirley Chisholm. She was running against Wallace for the presidential nomination. After the assassination attempt, Chisholm visited Wallace in the hospital despite strong opposition from her staff. She said, "Sometimes we have to remember we're all human beings, and I may be able to teach him something, to help him regain his humanity, to maybe make him open his eyes to make him see something that he has not seen. . . . One act of kindness may make all the difference in the world."[8] Peggie Wallace Kennedy recounted that

---

.washingtonpost.com/opinions/2019/05/16/changed-minds-reconciliation-voices-movement-episode/?

6. Colman McCarthy, "George Wallace—From the Heart," *Washington Post*, March 17, 1995, https://www.washingtonpost.com/wp-srv/politics/daily/sept98/wallace031795.htm.

7. Capeheart, "Wallace Became a Model for Racial Reconciliation."

8. Capeheart, "Wallace Became a Model for Racial Reconciliation."

her father was moved by Chisholm's "willingness to face the potential negative consequences of her political career because of him—something he had never done for anyone else."[9] The sacrificial act of love on the part of Chisholm set the stage for God to bring an amazing change of heart.

A costly act of empathetic lament opened a door for a seemingly impossible change of heart.

God Will Make It Right

The final hope is directly connected to the future. As we learned earlier in this book, all laments are designed to lead us to a renewed trust in God. We move from turning, complaining, and asking in order to conclude in trusting. This last step stakes our claim on God's faithfulness.

Lament connects our present challenges to the promise of future judgment.

Christians long for a future day when Jesus will return, truth will be known, and perfect justice delivered. It is precisely this hope which drives the psalmist to refuse to give in to despair. The lamenter turns to God with the hope that he will make it right:

> Give to them according to their work
> > and according to the evil of their deeds;
> give to them according to the work of their hands;
> > render them their due reward. (Ps. 28:4)

> I know that the LORD will maintain the cause of the afflicted,
> > and will execute justice for the needy. (Ps. 140:12)

> Steadfast love and faithfulness meet;
> > righteousness and peace kiss each other.
> Faithfulness springs up from the ground,
> > and righteousness looks down from the sky. (Ps. 85:10–11)

---

9. Capeheart, "Wallace Became a Model for Racial Reconciliation."

This hope-filled perspective is rooted in the gospel and essential for endurance. The gospel reminds us that our individual and collective sinfulness can be forgiven through the sacrifice of Jesus. Our judgment has been satisfied in Christ, and there is a coming day when God will settle all accounts. This becomes the basis of what it means for God to "make it right." John Piper, in *Bloodlines*, writes:

> I believe that the gospel—the good news of Christ crucified in our place to remove the wrath of God and provide forgiveness of sins and power for sanctification—is our only hope for the kind of racial diversity and harmony that ultimately matters. If we abandon the fullness of the gospel to make racial and ethnic diversity quicker or easier, we create a mere shadow of the kingdom, an imitation.[10]

There can be no understanding of justice apart from the cross.

But this is not merely a theological issue. There are hopeful implications that connect to how we live right now. Living out the gospel with a view toward God's future judgment means that we can be free from bitterness and the need to take revenge—either in our words or in our actions—while working to bring change.

Christians, therefore, don't sit on the sidelines—especially with complicated issues like racial reconciliation. We engage precisely because we know what's wrong with the world, what the solution is, and where it's all headed.

This applies to every Christian of every ethnicity. But in this chapter, I want to encourage my weary-hearted minority readers who have already borne so much pain. I'm pleading with you to keep helping the church understand the need for racial reconciliation. I want you to dare to hope that change can really happen. And when it is difficult and exhausting, I hope you'll continue to stay in the conversation as you apply the truth of 1 Peter: "When he was reviled, he did not revile in

---

10. John Piper, *Bloodlines: Race, Cross, and the Christian* (Wheaton, IL: Crossway, 2011), 40.

return; when he suffered, he did not threaten, but continued entrusting himself to him who judges justly" (1 Pet. 2:23).

I want to call you to be named among minority believers throughout the centuries who dared to keep hoping that change would come.

Small Victories

I'm happy to tell you that Aaron is not the only person who is experiencing the grace of reconciliation in our church. Our body of believers is not a model by any stretch. I'm navigating my way through how to lead a congregation to reflect the gospel not only in our beliefs but also in our practice. But every once in a while, we get a glimpse of the uniqueness of what can happen.

Keith is a black member of our church. I mentioned his wife, Yolanda, earlier in this book. They have been pioneers—even missionaries—in trying to help our church grow in ethnic harmony. They've been patient, trying to balance grace and truth over the years. Keith sent me an email detailing the effects of our church's efforts on the streets of Indianapolis. Here's what he wrote:

> I wanted to tell you about unity at College Park Church that extends to the streets of Indianapolis. Curt is a white Indianapolis Police officer (IMPD). I'm an African-American sheriff. We are brothers, and we get along well. Our families have fellowshipped together outside the church, and we have found ourselves working together on the streets. At one point recently we were at 40th and Winthrop. Shots were fired, and there were issues with juveniles. After things settled down, officers were all standing around talking in our divided circles.
>
> Curt stepped forward and gave me a brotherly hug in front of everyone. He said, "Hi, brother!" I reciprocated. I could see the wonder and puzzled look in the other officers' faces. Historically IMPD and the Sheriff Department have not worked well with each other. And, as you know, our two ethnic cultures have issues

too. Curt told me that afterwards some of the officers asked him, "What was that about?" He took the opportunity to explain that we were brothers in Christ. Curt and I are working to do what you are preaching about. It's good to see people notice.[11]

In order for racial reconciliation to take root, we must continue to pray and work for small victories not only in the church but also on the streets. The work of biblical unity is slow and costly. But if we continue together—locked arm in arm in the gospel—change is possible.

Progress, however, requires risk. That's especially true for minority Christians. And I hope that you continue to stay in the conversation and lead the way.

The gospel compels us to dare to hope.

◊

LAMENT PRAYER

Father, we're coming to you only because we know that we *should*. Honestly, praying about these issues, *again*, feels like a chore. If we've run out of the energy it takes to even believe things can change, how can you expect us to keep working for it? How long will we be forced to only *hear* of your goodness while we *see* the world's badness—particularly as these walls of racial pride, socio-economic injustice, and ethnic divisions not only continue to stand but are strengthened? How long will these reasons to despair surround us? How long will you require us to be people of hope, without giving us a foretaste of the unity you've promised? How long will the ignorant and apathetic hold the most influence in directing the affairs of your people? O God, the Creator of words who created with words, how long will you allow misunderstandings to be the

---

11. Edited email from Keith White, March 17, 2019, used by permission.

norm among your people? Why do you require your weary people to involve themselves in justice work that isn't working?

Father, give us reasons to hope again. Evict our most well-founded suspicions and replace them with undying trust of our brothers and sisters. Give us eyes to see the potential that lies in the mustard seeds of empathy and attempts at understanding. Make us the people of hope that truly reflect our belief in the resurrection. Remind us that with you there are no wasted efforts.

Our Lord, we know that you don't change. Your past faithfulness is the best indicator of your future work. Would you revive your work in *our* days? Would you come with power and renew our Spirits to keep moving forward in this work of seeing your church unified?

John Onwuchekwa,
pastor of Cornerstone Church,
Atlanta, Georgia

Discussion Questions

1. What was encouraging to you about the story with Aaron?

2. How might that story be different if the black leaders had responded with less grace and maturity?

3. In what ways have you experienced the risk of "daring to hope"?

4. What kinds of grace can God provide that might be unique to conversations connected to racial reconciliation?

5. How have you seen hardship produce transformation in other areas of your spiritual life? List some examples of how that can also be true when it comes to racial harmony.

6. If you were seated in the audience of Dexter Avenue Baptist Church, what do you think your response would be to Governor Wallace's confession?

7. In what areas have you seen your heart softened by reading this book?

8. How do the gospel and the hope of future judgment free believers to be kind and work for change?

Conclusion

LAMENT

An Open Door for Racial Reconciliation

Weep with those who weep. Live in harmony with one another.

ROMANS 12:15–16

My wife and I were enjoying a meal at a restaurant, but then what happened next to us was outrageous. An older white man repeatedly talked with gruff condescension to a black waitress as she attempted to take his order. When the meal wasn't exactly correct (his soup was actually too big!), he berated her. Every time she attempted to serve him or correct his order, he spoke with disdain. It was awful. It clearly affected the waitress. She walked away frustrated and hurt. The manager took her place serving the man.

While I don't know the condition of the man's heart, I was deeply grieved at his treatment of the waitress. It was hard not to sense an air of superiority and prejudice in how he talked. After we paid our bill, I circled our section to find the waitress. "Excuse me, ma'am," I said.

"I couldn't help hearing how you were treated by the man seated next to us. I want to commend you for your graciousness. And I want to give you something—a tip—just to say 'thank you.'"

The waitress fought back tears. She called for the manager—a white man. "Tell him," she said to me through her pain. I recounted the rude behavior to the manager. "She was very gracious," I said. The waitress jumped in, "I told you! I told you." The frustration and relief in her voice was obvious. The manager had apparently minimized the conflict. He expressed gratitude for helping him understand what happened, and the waitress pulled another person over and recounted the story.

As I walked away, our waiter caught me. He was a tall, young, black man. "Hey," he said, "that was cool, man."

I'm not sharing this story to impress you. In fact, at a forum on racial reconciliation, after I told this story, someone asked me why I didn't confront the white man. I said, "I'm not sure. Perhaps I should have. I kind of wish I had." So, please know I'm no model of courage.

But I am different today.

As I've lamented the history of racism, the complicity of the church, the division between believers, and the consequences of injustice for minority brothers and sisters, it birthed a compelling desire to advocate for racial harmony. A few years ago, I would not have processed the incident at the restaurant as I do now. I'm fairly sure I would not have felt compelled to do anything.

This story merely illustrates how what I see and hear has changed as I've learned to lament.

I trust the same has happened—or is starting to happen—for you.

The Vision

Our journey began with a familiar refrain: "I want the church to look more like heaven."

I don't know any Christians who think the future, heavenly vision of ethnic unity in Revelation 7 is a bad idea. In fact, I don't think you can claim to be a follower of Jesus and object to that vision. The issue, however, relates to what steps we can take now. This is where tension, misunderstanding, and missteps close the door quickly. Michael Emerson and Christian Smith, in *Divided by Faith*, summarize the problem well: "Evangelicals desire to end racial division and inequality, and attempt to think and act accordingly. But, in the process, they likely do more to perpetuate the racial divide than they do to tear it down."[1] In other words, most Christians are not sure what to do. Sure, there are some whose hearts are sinfully closed and hardened. But I think most Christians simply lack the tools. Dhati Lewis says, "We know something is wrong, but we don't feel we have the means necessary to bring change."[2]

The aim of this book has been to demonstrate how lament has the potential to move Christians of different ethnicities toward harmony. Instead of our cultural narratives, political talking points, and arguments about history, the biblical prayer language of lament strikes a different posture and tone.

Lament is flexible and fluid enough for both minority and majority Christians. In part 2, I explained the way lament could be helpful for majority-culture Christians as we empathize, end our silence, and repent where necessary. In part 3, we learned how lament serves minority Christians as they lovingly protest the evil, redeem their hurt, and dare to hope for change. As we love, listen, lament, learn, and leverage together, lament can be a turning point in the racial-reconciliation process.

Lament isn't a silver bullet. It doesn't solve all problems. In the same way that there are fears and a sense of inadequacy when helping a friend who is grieving a loss, the nature of this pain might cause you to distance yourself or jump in too quickly with unhelpful solutions.

---

1. Michael Emerson and Christian Smith, *Divided by Faith: Evangelical Religion and the Problem of Race in America* (New York: Oxford University Press, 2000), ix.

2. Dhati Lewis, *Advocates: The Narrow Path to Racial Reconciliation* (Nashville: B&H, 2019), loc. 649 of 1987, Kindle.

What's true in grief is also true in racial reconciliation: lament helps. It's a tool—a step in the right direction.

Even though we come from different experiences and emotions, the biblical language of processing pain (turning, complaining, asking, and trusting) opens the door for renewed understanding and love.

But it also creates a pathway for healing and a prophetic call for change.

What's Next?

Lament isn't a destination. It moves you from where you are to where you need to be. Lament is necessary, but it is never enough.

Isaac Adams, the host of the *United? We Pray* podcast, says, "When it comes to racial reconciliation, we must do more than pray; but we cannot do less."[3] Prayer is essential, but there's more to do. I've addressed a wide array of applications throughout this book. Let me give you a few final suggestions at a personal and corporate level.

Personal

What's your role in bridging the gap in racial reconciliation? Hopefully you've asked yourself this question throughout the book. Even more, I trust you now have a greater desire to be part of the solution. Here's what you might consider next.

Rehearse the biblical vision. Use the Bible to fuel your passion. Read the vision for unity in Revelation 7:9–12. Memorize Paul's words about Christian identity in Colossians 3:5–11. Meditate on the unity purchased by Jesus in Ephesians 2. Regularly rehearse God's vision for reconciliation.

Practice lament. Take time to read the lament psalms. Explore how they express sorrow through prayer. Practice applying the language of lament, and then direct it to racial reconciliation—whether in processing your hurt, communicating you care, or protesting the brokenness of the world.

---

3. Isaac Adams, "Lament in Indianapolis," interview with Mark Vroegop, October 9, 2019, *United? We Pray*, produced by Josh Deng, podcast, 13:44, https://uwepray.com/feed/0402.

Build relationships. Empathy isn't possible from a distance. Developing relationships with people of different ethnicities is essential. Hospitality and friendship create the venue for Christian love to be expressed and pain to be understood. Don't wait for reconciliation to come to you. Be the initiator—like Jesus was to you.

Grow in your understanding. Consider reading books on racial reconciliation, especially from people outside your "tribe." Learning the history, layers, and background of the issues will create more competency in engaging with conversations. Use social media to follow how particular leaders process racially loaded incidents and topics. Take time to understand both sides of an issue. Learn the definitions. Look for the layers. Learn how to interpret an issue from a different perspective.

Engage where you are. Determine what steps you can take to be an advocate for ethnic harmony. Perhaps it's as simple as speaking up when someone says something inappropriate or prejudiced. Maybe you could engage in your community's wrestling with issues rooted in historic injustice. Or you might feel led to use your financial resources to express your commitment.

Don't stop. My list is surely not complete. You'll need to prayerfully wrestle with the steps God is calling you to take. As you learn to lament the barriers to racial reconciliation, you'll begin to see doors of opportunity. And when the Lord opens them, I hope you'll find ways to take personal steps toward harmony.

Corporate

Beyond personal steps that move us toward biblical unity, it's important for groups of people, especially churches, to embrace the opportunity to build racial harmony. What are some ways lament and racial reconciliation can be applied corporately?

Teach biblical unity in diversity. Christians need to be taught the importance of racial harmony. If you have a teaching role—in your family, small group, Sunday school, or worship services—consider how you can invite people to embrace the biblical goal of a unified church. Help people around you see the beautiful picture of "Christ [as] all, and in all" (Col. 3:11).

Model lament. Lament is the biblical language of corporate grief. It's how the people of God mourn the brokenness of the world. Therefore, Christians need to be taught how to lament. For most believers, this is not a familiar prayer language. But as we learn how to apply it to the common griefs of life, it isn't hard to see its usefulness in racial reconciliation. Teach people how to be competent lamenters. And then model it.

Mourn together at critical moments. When a racially charged incident breaks on the news, minority friends and church members might wonder if you've seen what's transpired. But they could also wonder if you care. Taking time in a small group or in a pastoral prayer to lament over an event—even as it continues to unfold and the truth comes to light—communicates your awareness, sensitivity, and concern. It also serves to remind the entire church about our collective need to "weep with those who weep." In this way, lament encourages people to lean toward one another when an incident would incline you to take opposite sides or keep your distance.

Create venues for dialogue. I've personally witnessed the value of forums, discussion groups, and pilgrimages for progress. Consider starting a discussion group that explores the issues and barriers in this conversation. Perhaps you could host a forum where someone provides teaching or recounts an experience and allow time for dialogue. Additionally, I've found the Civil Rights Vision Trip to be incredibly strategic.[4] This annual pilgrimage combines learning, relationship, and experience in a deeply transformative way. If a three- or four-day trip is not possible, consider a shorter trip to a historic location to learn and lament together.

---

4. See appendix 3 for a sample itinerary.

Intentionally celebrate and create diversity. Take the opportunity to pray or partner with churches whose ethnic demographic is different from yours. Consider a joint prayer meeting, or swapping preachers or music teams for a Sunday. Host a lunch for pastors of different ethnicities to spend time together. If you're in a position of leadership, think through how to bring ethnic diversity to your church, worship style, and leadership. The church needs the voices and perspectives of people who do not look the same.

Advocate for change. Depending on your location and demographic, this will look different in each church. But do what you can to help your church to look a little more like heaven. Corporate change is slow and complicated. You'll need wisdom to not outpace the people of your church or move too slowly out of fear. But I've seen the gospel-shaped beauty of people from different ethnicities loving one another.

It's not easy. It's often complicated. But it's worth it.

And I've seen the way lament has helped.

Open Doors

As you have walked through this book and learned to lament, I hope you have felt a sense of calling to pursue reconciliation. The journey is not without risk. It can get messy. Be prepared to shed some tears. But you now know a language for navigating the challenging territory of this conversation. The church desperately needs competent lamenters in the cause of racial reconciliation.

We don't need to wait until heaven for unity.

God's plan for the church has always involved an unexplainable oneness. Jesus purchased it. In this respect, reconciliation is not something we need to create. It's already accomplished through the gospel. Unfortunately, sin continues to mar the harmony of the church. That's why we must lean into this conversation.

While there are many steps to take, the least we can do is mourn together over the brokenness that creates so much division and hurt. We can talk to God and allow the historic language of sorrow to pull us together. We need to help the church look more like what Jesus intended—right now.

Weeping with those who weep opens a door for reconciliation. For the sake of the witness of the church and the validation of the gospel, we should mourn. Lament doesn't solve everything. But it's a good place to start.

I've seen it. I've felt it. I hope you have too.

Come, brothers and sisters, let's weep together so we can live in harmony—together.

◊

LAMENT PRAYER

O Father—*our* Father—so many of your children see racial strife. We hear it. We suffer under it. And yet, Lord, too many of your children don't acknowledge the reality of ethnic partiality. And still we perpetuate it.

God, how can this be? How can so many of our churches and lives be willfully segregated? How can a callous individualism mark a people who are supposed to be one in Christ?

God, we thank you for the racial progress that has been made. But sometimes it seems your gospel conquers everything *but* race. That can't be, O Lord!

And yet, Father, it often seems like we're far from that Revelation vision where every tribe is united around your throne. Instead, it feels like we're at Babel: we're together, but we're fighting; we're talking, but we're speaking different languages past one another. O Lord, with the frustration among us, it seems your churches are under your judgment still.

But, Lord, we now look away from the division behind us and in front of us. We turn to you with *our* grief by *your* grace. O

God, would you give us grace to cherish Christ more deeply, and to remember how your judgment has fallen on him *instead* of us! Help us to sincerely live as what you've made us in Christ: one new man—a chosen race—that the world may believe you sent your Son.

Until Babel is completely undone, we beg for your help in Jesus's name, amen.

Isaac Adams,
assistant pastor of Capitol Hill Baptist Church,
Washington, DC,
host of *United? We Pray*

Discussion Questions

1. Before reading this book, what were your attitudes and perspectives related to racial reconciliation?

2. How has your thinking changed?

3. What are the biggest revelations? What created the change?

4. What remaining questions are you still working through?

5. Make a list of three specific steps you will take, personally and corporately, after reading this book.

6. Develop an answer to this question: Why should I care about racial reconciliation?

7. Write out a prayer of lament in light of the content of this book. Consider sharing it with a friend, in a small group, or on social media.

8. Develop a prayer list of people in your sphere of relationships who come from different ethnicities.

Appendix 1

PSALMS OF LAMENT

Personal An individual vocalizing pain, grief, fear, or some other strong emotion	3, 4, 5, 7, 10, 13, 17, 22, 25, 26, 28, 31, 39, 42, 43, 54, 55, 56, 57, 59, 61, 64, 70, 71, 77, 86, 120, 141, 142
Corporate A group or nation vocalizing pain, grief, fear, or some other strong emotion	12, 44, 58, 60, 74, 79, 80, 83, 85, 90, 94, 123, 126
Repentant An individual or group expressing regret or sorrow for sin	6, 32, 38, 51, 102, 130, 143
Imprecatory An individual or group expressing outrage and a strong desire for justice	35, 69, 83, 88, 109, 137, 140
Partial Sections of lament within other psalms	9:13–20; 27:7–14; 40:11–17
Debatable Psalms that some consider to be lament in total or in part	14, 36, 41, 52, 53, 63, 78, 81, 89, 106, 125, 129, 139*

* Rosann Catalano, "How Long, O Lord? A Systematic Study of the Theology and Practice of Biblical Lament" (doctoral diss., Toronto School of Theology, 1988), 59; Dennis Bratcher, "Types of Psalms," Christian Resource Institute: The Voice, accessed January 30, 2018, http://www.crivoice.org/psalmtypes.html.

Appendix 2

LEARNING-TO-LAMENT WORKSHEET

Movements of Lament	Psalm ___	My Lament
Turn to God Address God as you come to him in prayer. This is sometimes combined with complaint.		
Bring Your Complaint Identify in blunt language the specific pain or injustice. *Why* or *how* is often part of the complaint.		
Ask Boldly Specifically call upon God to act in a manner that fits his character and resolves your complaint.		
Choose to Trust Affirm God's worthiness to be trusted, and commit to praising him.		

Learning-to-Lament Worksheet, Sample 1

Movements of Lament	Psalm 86	My Lament
Turn to God Address God as you come to him in prayer. This is sometimes combined with complaint.	v. 1: "Incline your ear, O LORD, and answer me, / for I am poor and needy." v. 6; "Give ear, O LORD, to my prayer; / listen to my plea for grace."	God, I need you to hear me. I'm hurting and in pain. I'm asking for you to listen to my lament. I desperately need your grace today.
Bring Your Complaint Identify in blunt language the specific pain or injustice. *Why* or *how* is often part of the complaint.	v. 14: "O God, insolent men have risen up against me; / a band of ruthless men seeks my life, / and they do not set you before them."	You've heard every unfair word, and you know how I've been misunderstood. I'm upset. I'm defensive. I want to strike back with more words. I don't feel like they care. It doesn't end. I don't know what to do.

Movements of Lament	Psalm 86	My Lament
Ask Boldly Specifically call upon God to act in a manner that fits his character and resolves your complaint.	v. 2: "Preserve my life . . . / save your servant." v. 3: "Be gracious to me, O Lord." v. 11: "Teach me your way, O LORD . . . / unite my heart to fear your name." v. 16: "Turn to me and be gracious to me; / give your strength to your servant." v. 17: "Show me a sign of your favor."	Teach me every lesson you want me to learn through this. Help me know what to say or not to say. Make my heart love your purposes more than I love my reputation. Help me know that you are listening and that you care for me. I need help, God. My heart is so divided. One minute I think good thoughts. The next, ugly thoughts. Pour out your grace on me, please!
Choose to Trust Affirm God's worthiness to be trusted, and commit to praising him.	v. 8: "There is none like you among the gods, O Lord." v. 12: "I give thanks to you, O Lord my God, with my whole heart." v. 13: "Great is your steadfast love." v. 15: "But you, O Lord, are a God merciful and gracious, / slow to anger and abounding in steadfast love and faithfulness" v. 17: "You, LORD, have helped me and comforted me."	None of this is a surprise to you. You've heard every word. You know what I'm feeling, and you are greater than anything I face. You can supply what I need and give me the strength if others don't understand. I can trust you with what people say about me. You've helped me through many worse situations. So I'm going to keep my eyes on you. I'm trusting you. I'm still going to worship you. Thank you.

SAMPLE CIVIL RIGHTS VISION TRIP ITINERARY

Day 1: Thursday—Travel and Birmingham, AL

6:00 a.m. (EDT)	Travel from College Park Church
11:00 a.m. (CDT)	Find lunch around truck stop
12:00 p.m.	Travel to Birmingham, AL (lament session 1)
2:30 p.m.	16th Street Baptist Church and tour
	Walk across the street to the Birmingham Civil Rights Institute
3:30 p.m.	Birmingham Civil Rights Institute and tour
5:00 p.m.	Travel to dinner sites
6:15 p.m.	Travel to hotel in Birmingham
7:00 p.m.	Debrief the day
8:00 p.m.	Free Time

Day 2: Friday—Montgomery and Selma, AL

7:30 a.m.	Travel from hotel in Birmingham (lament session 2)
9:00 a.m.	The National Memorial for Peace and Justice, Montgomery, AL
11:45 a.m.	Walk to the Legacy Museum
12:00 p.m.	Find lunch around the Legacy Museum
1:00 p.m.	The Legacy Museum and tour

2:00 p.m.	Other sites:
	Alabama State Capitol
	Dexter Avenue Baptist Church
	Rosa Parks bus stop
	Market Street and Court Square Fountain (site of slave auction)
	Juliette Hampton Morgan Memorial Library
	Meet back at the bus at the Legacy Museum
3:00 p.m.	Travel to Selma, AL
5:00 p.m.	Walk Edmund Pettus Bridge
5:30 p.m.	Travel to hotel in Selma
6:15 p.m.	Dinner in Selma
8:45 p.m.	Travel to hotel in Selma

Day 3: Saturday—Selma, AL; Marks, MS; and Clarksdale, MS

7:00 a.m.	Travel from hotel in Selma (lament session 3)
12:00 p.m.	Lunch
1:00 p.m.	Travel to various sites:
	Site of Mule Train launch of Poor People's March
	Shady Grove Cemetery
	Marks Cemetery
	Cotton field
	Aaron Henry's home
5:00 p.m.	Dinner in Clarksdale
7:30 p.m.	Travel to hotel in Greenwood

Day 4: Sunday—Greenwood and Memphis Travel

9:00 a.m.	Travel from hotel in Greenwood
9:15 a.m.	Emmett Till historical marker
10:15 a.m.	Travel to local Missionary Baptist Church
11:00 a.m.	Local Missionary Baptist Church service
1:30 p.m.	Lunch in Greenwood
3:00 p.m.	Travel to Memphis (lament session 4)

5:00 p.m.	Check in at hotel in Memphis
5:30 p.m.	Dinner near hotel

Day 5: Monday—Memphis and Return

8:30 a.m.	Travel from hotel in Memphis
9:00 a.m.	Lorraine Motel and National Civil Rights Museum and tour
12:00 p.m.	Lunch
1:00 p.m.	Depart Lorraine Motel and National Civil Rights Museum (lament session 5)
5:00 p.m.	Find food around truck stop
6:00 p.m. (CDT)	Travel to College Park Church
10:00 p.m. (EDT)	Arrive at College Park Church

BIBLIOGRAPHY

Allen, Richard. "A Prayer for Hope." In *Conversations with God: Two Centuries of Prayers by African Americans*, edited by James Melvin Washington, 10. New York: HarperCollins, 1994.

Anyabwile, Thabiti. "He Said, She Said." The Gospel Coalition. April 12, 2018. https://www.thegospelcoalition.org/blogs/thabiti-anyabwile/he -said-she-said/.

The Archaeological Encyclopedia of the Holy Land. Edited by Avraham Negev. 3rd ed. New York: Prentice Hall, 1990.

Austin, Benjamin M., and Jonathan Sutter. "Exile." In *Lexham Theological Wordbook*, edited by Douglas Mangum, Derek R. Brown, and Rachel Klippenstein. Lexham Bible Reference Series. Bellingham, WA: Lexham, 2014.

Bruce, James. "Should We Apologize for Sins We Did Not Commit?" The Gospel Coalition. July 14, 2016. https://www.thegospelcoalition.org /article/should-we-apologize-for-sins-we-did-not-commit/.

Capeheart, Jonathan. "How Segregationist George Wallace Became a Model for Racial Reconciliation: 'Voices of the Movement' Episode 6." *Washington Post.* May 16, 2015. https://www.washington post.com/opinions/2019/05/16/changed-minds-reconciliation-voices -movement-episode/?.

Card, Michael. *A Sacred Sorrow: Reaching Out to God in the Lost Language of Lament.* Colorado Springs: NavPress, 2005.

Chenu, Bruno. *The Trouble I've Seen: The Big Book of Negro Spirituals.* Valley Forge, PA: Judson, 2003.

Edmondson, Mika. "Hopeful Strategies for Hard Conversations." The Gospel Coalition. April 5, 2019. https://www.thegospelcoalition.org/conference_media/hopeful-strategies-hard-conversations/.

Edmondson, Mika. "Is Black Lives Matter the New Civil Rights Movement?" The Gospel Coalition. June 24, 2016. https://www.the gospelcoalition.org/article/is-black-lives-matter-the-new-civil-rights -movement/.

Elliott, Debbie. "How a Mule Train from Marks, Miss., Kicked Off MLK's Poor People Campaign." NPR (website). May 13, 2018. https://www .npr.org/2018/05/13/610097454/how-a-mule-train-from-marks-miss -kicked-off-mlks-poor-people-campaign.

Emerson, Michael, and Christian Smith. *Divided by Faith: Evangelical Religion and the Problem of Race in America.* New York: Oxford University Press, 2000.

Estes, Daniel J. *Psalms 73–150.* Vol. 13 of *The New American Commentary.* Nashville: B&H, 2019.

ESV Study Bible. Edited by Wayne Grudem, J. I. Packer, C. John Collins, and Thomas R. Schreiner. Wheaton, IL: Crossway, 2008.

Faithful, George. "Recovering the Theology of the Negro Spiritual." *Credo ut Intelligam.* December 13, 2007. https://theologyjournal .wordpress.com/2007/12/13/recovering-the-theology-of-the-negro -spirituals/.

Hall, Matthew. "The Historical Causes of the Stain of Racism in the Southern Baptist Convention." In *Removing the Stain of Racism from the Southern Baptist Convention: Diverse African American and White Perspectives,* edited by Jarvis J. Williams and Kevin M. Jones, 7–14. Nashville: B&H, 2017.

Hill, Daniel. *White Awake: An Honest Look at What It Means to Be White.* Downers Grove, IL: InterVarsity Press, 2017.

Hunter, Drew. *Made for Friendship: The Relationship That Halves Our Sorrows and Doubles Our Joys.* Wheaton, IL: Crossway, 2018.

Jacobs, Harriet [Linda Brent, pseud.]. *Incidents in the Life of a Slave Girl.* Fairford, UK: Echo Library Classics, 2011.

Jones, Arthur C. *Wade in the Water: The Wisdom of the Spirituals.* New York: Orbis, 1993.

"Juliette Hampton Morgan, 1914–1957." Civil Rights Digital Library. Accessed July 17, 2019. http://crdl.usg.edu/people/m/morgan_juliette _hampton_1914_1957/.

King, Martin Luther, Jr. "'I Have a Dream,' Address Delivered at the March on Washington for Jobs and Freedom." Martin Luther King, Jr. Research and Education Institute, Stanford University. Accessed April 26, 2019. https://kinginstitute.stanford.edu/king-papers/documents/i -have-dream-address-delivered-march-washington-jobs-and-freedom.

King, Martin Luther, Jr. "Letter from a Birmingham Jail—April 16, 1963." Martin Luther King, Jr. Research and Education Institute, Stanford University. Accessed June 14, 2019. http://okra.stanford.edu /transcription/document_images/undecided/630416-019.pdf.

King, Martin Luther, Jr. "Where Do We Go from Here? Address Delivered at the Eleventh Annual SCLC Convention, August 16, 1967." Martin Luther King, Jr. Research and Education Institute, Stanford University. Accessed September 13, 2019. https://kinginstitute.stanford .edu/king-papers/documents/where-do-we-go-here-address-delivered -eleventh-annual-sclc-convention.

Kennedy, Robert. "Statement on Assassination of Martin Luther King, Jr., Indianapolis, Indiana, April 4, 1968." John F. Kennedy Presidential Library and Museum. Accessed May 16, 2019. https://www.jfklibrary .org/learn/about-jfk/the-kennedy-family/robert-f-kennedy/robert-f -kennedy-speeches/statement-on-assassination-of-martin-luther-king -jr-indianapolis-indiana-april-4-1968.

Lewis, Dhati. *Advocates: The Narrow Path to Racial Reconciliation.* Nashville: B&H, 2019.

Loritts, Bryan. "Don't just be prophetic in your denunciations of racism, also be pastoral." Twitter, April 12, 2019, 12:56 p.m. https://twitter .com/bcloritts/status/1116792293187436544.

Loritts, Bryan. *Insider Outsider: My Journey as a Stranger in White Evangelicalism and My Hope for Us All.* Grand Rapids, MI: Zondervan, 2018.

Mason, Eric. "How Should the Church Engage?" In *The Gospel and Racial Reconciliation*, edited by Russell Moore and Andrew T. Walker, 53–68. Nashville: B&H, 2016.

Mason, Eric. *Woke Church: An Urgent Call for Christians in America to Confront Racism and Injustice.* Chicago: Moody Publishers, 2018.

McCarthy, Colman. "George Wallace—From the Heart." *Washington Post.* March 17, 1995. https://www.washingtonpost.com/wp-srv/politics /daily/sept98/wallace031795.htm.

"Memorial." EJI (The National Memorial for Peace and Justice website). Accessed May 16, 2019. https://museumandmemorial.eji.org /memorial.

Meyer, Jason. "How the Gospel Turns Racial Apathy into Empathy." The Gospel Coalition. July 15, 2016. https://www.thegospelcoalition.org /article/how-gospel-turns-racial-apathy-into-empathy/.

Meyer, Jason. "Trusting God in the Darkest Night." Bethlehem Baptist Church (website), July 10, 2016. https://bethlehem.church/sermon /trusting-god-in-the-darkest-night/.

Moore, Russell. "King and Kingdom: Racial Justice and the Uneasy Conscience of American Christianity." Russell Moore (blog). April 10, 2018. https://www.russellmoore.com/2018/04/10/king-and-kingdom -racial-justice-and-the-uneasy-conscience-of-american-christianity/.

Newman, Richard. *Go Down, Moses: Celebrating the African-American Spiritual.* New York: Clarkson Potter, 1998.

Perkins, John. *One Blood: Parting Words to the Church on Race and Love.* Chicago: Moody Publishers, 2018.

Piper, John. *Bloodlines: Race, Cross, and the Christian.* Wheaton, IL: Crossway, 2011.

Polhill, John B. *Acts.* Vol. 26 of *The New American Commentary.* Nashville: Broadman & Holman, 1992.

Raboteau, Albert J. *Slave Religion: The "Invisible Institution" in the Antebellum South.* Oxford: Oxford University Press, 2004.

Rah, Soong-Chan. *Prophetic Lament: A Call for Justice in Troubled Times.* Downers Grove, IL: InterVarsity Press, 2015.

"Resolution on Racial Reconciliation on the 150th Anniversary of the Southern Baptist Convention, Atlanta, Georgia—1995." Southern Baptist Convention (website). http://www.sbc.net/resolutions/899 /resolution-on-racial-reconciliation-on-the-150th-anniversary-of-the -southern-baptist-convention.

Rosenwald, Michael. "That Stain of Bloodshed: After King's Assassination, RFK Calmed an Angry Crowd with an Unforgettable Speech." *Washington Post*, April 4, 2018. https://www.washingtonpost.com /news/retropolis/wp/2018/04/03/that-stain-of-bloodshed-after-kings -assassination-rfk-calmed-an-angry-crowd-with-an-unforgettable -speech.

"Slavery in America." History (website). November 12, 2009. https://www .history.com/topics/black-history/slavery.

"Sometimes I Feel Like a Motherless Child." Hymnary (website). Accessed April 26, 2019. https://hymnary.org/text/sometimes_i_feel_like _a_motherless_child.

"The Speech." Kennedy King Memorial Initiative. Accessed May 16, 2019. http://kennedykingindy.org/thespeech.

Stark, Rodney. *The Rise of Christianity: How the Obscure, Marginal Jesus Movement Became the Dominant Religious Force in the Western World in a Few Centuries*. New York: HarperOne, 1996.

Stetzer, Ed. "It's Time to Listen: Feeling the Pain Despite the Facts, a Guest Post by Bryan Loritts." *Christianity Today*. August 20, 2014. https://www.christianitytoday.com/edstetzer/2014/august/its-time-to -listen.html.

Storms, Sam. "Is It Possible to Repent for the Sins of Others?" Sam Storms, Enjoying God (blog). November 23, 2015. https://www.sam storms.org/enjoying-god-blog/post/is-it-possible-to-repent-for-the -sins-of-others.

Thurman, Howard. *Deep River and the Negro Spiritual Speaks of Life and Death*. Richmond, IN: Friends United, 1975.

Tisby, Jemar. *The Color of Compromise: The Truth about the American Church's Complicity in Racism*. Grand Rapids, MI: Zondervan, 2019.

Tisby, Jemar. "How We Get Free: Faith in the Black Freedom Struggle." Lecture delivered at the University of Indianapolis, February 13, 2019.

Van Noord, Rebecca. "A Conversation with Hip Hop Artist and Preacher Trip Lee." *Bible Study Magazine.* July/August 2017. http://www.bible studymagazine.com/julyaugust-2017-trip-lee.

Washington, James Melvin. *Conversations with God: Two Centuries of Prayers by African Americans.* New York: HarperCollins, 1994.

West, Cornel. "The Spirituals as Lyric Poetry." In *The Cornel West Reader.* New York: Basic Civitas, 1999.

Wilkerson, Isabel. *The Warmth of Other Suns: The Epic Story of America's Great Migration.* New York: Vintage, 2010.

Williams, Reggie. *Bonhoeffer's Black Jesus: Harlem Renaissance Theology and an Ethic of Resistance.* Waco, TX: Baylor University Press, 2014.

GENERAL INDEX

SCRIPTURE INDEX

Also Available
from Mark Vroegop

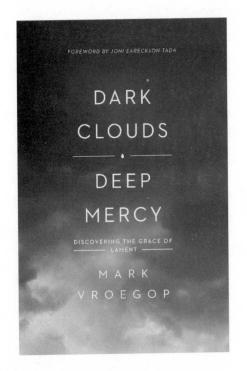

2020 ECPA Christian Book of the Year®

"If you are going through hard times, this book may provide more insight and comfort than any other book except for the Bible."

DONALD S. WHITNEY, author, *Family Worship*; *Spiritual Disciplines for the Christian Life*; and *Praying the Bible*

For more information, visit **crossway.org**.